THE BIG BOOK OF

CATHOLIC CUSTOMS AND TRADITIONS

for Children's Faith Formation

Edited by Beth Branigan McNamara
with Sue Robinson and Anne E. Neuberger

Our Sunday Visitor Publishing Division
Our Sunday Visitor, Inc.
Huntington, Indiana 46750

Our Sunday Visitor Publishing Division
Our Sunday Visitor, Inc.
200 Noll Plaza
Huntington, IN 46750

ISBN: 1-931709-44-0 (Inventory No. R26)

Cover and text design by Tyler Ottinger
Additional illustrations by Kevin Davidson, Brenda Anderson, Peggy Geradot, Margaret Zellhofer, and Carol Morris.

PRINTED IN THE UNITED STATES OF AMERICA

Contents

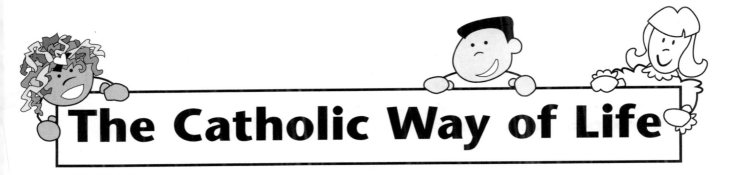

The Catholic Way of Life

The practice and celebration of religious customs and practices is a powerful way to experience the story of our Catholic Faith. Grounded in our long faith-tradition, they help us celebrate our beliefs and our Catholic identity. These opportunities inspired by the Holy Spirit give us the richness of God's grace in many forms. When teaching young children about religious symbols and traditional prayers, teachers and parents are giving children a connection between the child's religious expression and that of the adult's. What may be simply a subconscious awareness at age 3 becomes a full understanding as an adult. What they learn as young children is built up, and can be drawn from as they get older. In a similar vein, rituals and prayers learned as children can be comforting in times of grief or stress as adults. By teaching children our customs and traditions, new generations will continue to experience and embrace their Catholic Faith.

Religious Customs and Traditions Are Valuable
- They respond to our religious needs.
- They are repeated on a regular basis, deepening and reinforcing our faith.
- They take their form from the events of our daily lives, cultures, and experiences.
- They are experiential, engaging the heart, body, senses, environment, intuition, and imagination.
- They provide role-models of holiness, as we celebrate the lives of the Saints.
- They spark a child's prayer life, through prayer, devotion and blessing rituals.

This book offers teachers, parents and caregivers information, stories, legends, ideas, activities and crafts that will help children celebrate many of our religious feasts and seasons. Engaging children in these rich customs and practices will result in a deeper relationship with Jesus and a commitment to their faith.

This easy-to-use guide first introduces your children to everyday practices and then travels through the months of the year and Church seasons. Woven together with commonly celebrated holidays, they will provide grace-filled moments that pass on the richness of our Catholic Faith to future generations.

Beth Branigan McNamara
Sue Robinson
Anne E. Neuberger

Introduction

A Few Simple Keys to Sharing Customs and Traditions in the Classroom

1. Always be prepared and relaxed. Keep your voice level, soft and pleasant. Remember that your voice, gestures and mannerisms teach. If needed, take moments to pause, speak in a whisper or chant your directions. Always strive to be poised, calm and quiet.

2. Adapt the customs and traditions to your class. It's essential to keep in mind the ages of the children and adapt what you are doing to their level of development. Many of the customs, traditions and activities in this book can be adapted to a wide-range of age groups.

3. Always gain the children's attention before you begin. Seat less attentive and more active children near you.

4. Give very precise, simple and positive directions.

5. Listen and observe with your whole being: ears, mind and emotions (the children will learn to do the same).

6. Acknowledge and address all questions. This is how children learn. Give children definitions to difficult words, but don't be afraid to leave some questions of faith unanswered. This helps children to see that even adults ponder faith questions. As adults we call them mysteries of our faith.

Short and Simple Everyday Practices to Get You Started

Incorporate quick faith-building practices into your daily classroom routine to remind the children that Jesus is with us throughout all of our daily activities and that all of our actions should reflect Jesus' teaching. Good daily habits will help us build our friendship with Jesus and grow closer to God. Here are a few ideas to get you started!

- When you turn on a light, you say "Jesus, Light of the World."
- Take a few minutes before each meal to ask God to bless you and the food you are about to eat.
- Pray every night before you go to bed. Use this time to tell Jesus about your day. Give thanks for all the gifts (such as your family) that you have been blessed with and ask for forgiveness for the mistakes you have made.
- Remember to thank the Lord during the day for giving you all you have! A short and simple thank you will fill you with gratitude.
- While cleaning out your desk or washing tables or any other chores, pray for those who will benefit from the work that you are doing.
- When you pass a Catholic Church say, "Jesus, I love you!"
- When you hear the siren of an ambulance or fire engine, pray for the people who need help and for the safety of those coming to their aid.
- When you can't concentrate, say a prayer.
- When you can't sleep, say a prayer.

The Celebration (Prayer) Table

In addition to storytelling and activities, consider creating a "visual presence" in your classroom or home. One of many ways you can do this quite simply is by designating a corner, desk, or side table as your "Celebration Table."

This is a place for you and your children to be as artistic as you want. For a tablecloth, use colorful fabric that reflects the season. To begin, place a candle, a cross, an age-appropriate Bible, and an image of Jesus, perhaps as the Good Shepherd. For a saint day, display a holy card, statue or illustration from a saint book. Add symbols of this saint (i.e. for Thérèse the Little Flower, have tiny flowers in a vase; for St. Francis, add toy animals). For liturgical seasons, use the color used in church (i.e., for Advent, use violet.).

General Celebration Table Ideas
- A copy of an age-appropriate Bible
- Vigil lights
- Pictures of Jesus, Mary, Joseph, and/or other saints
- A church calendar
- A holy water font
- Several prayer mats on the floor

Activity: *Making Prayer Mats*

Carpet samples make perfect prayer rugs for children of all ages. Place a few around the celebration table for sitting or kneeling on. Leave the rugs blank or, using paint, stencil on a symbolic pattern such as a cross or print a phrase such as "Give Thanks." You might make a prayer rug for each child in your room printing, "(Child's name)'s Prayer Rug."

A Word About Legends

When learning of people who lived hundreds of years ago, it is difficult to differentiate between what is fact and what is fiction. However, many stories are based on fact that has been "embroidered" over the years, so which details happened and which didn't are impossible to sort. Also, even if the events in stories never actually happened at all, there are reasons that the story survived. Mainly this is because the story presents a truth about the person we should know, or that it reveals the person's relationship with God. This makes the story invaluable in itself. Stories teach on many levels, and legends are an important category of stories. In this book, you will find numerous saint stories that are based on legends, or on facts that cannot be verified. As we stand here, peering back into the shadowy past, must we try to judge? After all, a story either happened, or it holds a lesson so important, it has survived for hundreds of years. Either one is gift.

Liturgical Season Colors

Green, the color of hope and life, is used in Ordinary Time.

Purple is used for Advent; traditionally on the third Sunday of Advent, rose or pink to reflect anticipation for Christmas joy.

The Everyday

Purple is used during Lent, and special penitential days.

White is the color of the Easter season, Christmas season, feasts of our Lord and Mary, non-martyred saints, and special solemnities outside these times.

Red is used for Pentecost, Good Friday and feasts of martyrs.

Prayer

Living in the presence of God means making prayer the natural response to everything we do, from waking to sleeping, from playing to learning, from leaving to returning. Throughout our daily activities we are provided with countless opportunities to pray with our children. By making time to pray throughout our day and explaining why we do it, important prayerful habits are formed, and they begin to play a vital part in our children's lives. Jesus prayed daily, making this one of the earliest Catholic traditions. Daily Prayer is a way of sanctifying our lives, both day and night.

Traditional rote prayers are often learned by heart offering children an easy, comfortable way to pray at anytime. Teach memorized prayer slowly. Take each prayer apart, phrase by phrase, explaining and discussing the meaning of each phrase. When learning traditional prayer, never put a child on the spot. Repetition is the key to remembering the words.

Sign of the Cross

Upon entering the church, we dip our fingertips into the holy water and make the shape of the cross on ourselves. By doing this, we bless ourselves with water to remind us that we were baptized with water and are disciples of God's love.

The Sign of the Cross is made with the hand, touching first the forehead, then the breast, left shoulder, and finally the right shoulder. While doing it, it is common to add an expression of faith in the Trinity: "In the name of the Father, and of the Son, and of the Holy Spirit. Amen."

Activity: *My Heart, My Mind, My Actions*

Traditionally this sign has been used to begin and to complete prayer but also as a sign to God that we ask for God's presence:

In the name of the Father	*Be in my mind*
And of the Son	*Be in my heart*
And of the Holy Spirit.	*And in all of my actions*
Amen.	

Morning Prayer and Offering

Catholics are taught to begin each day with a prayer offering the frustrations and joys of the day to God for the building up of God's kingdom on earth.

Today Lord, [make the Sign of the Cross]
Open my eyes to see your goodness in all things.
Open my ears to hear the needs of others.
Open my mouth to speak words of kindness.
Open my mind to all I learn and experience.
Today Lord, be in my heart!

Blessed be God who gives us this new day!
May we be a reflection of Jesus in all we do, think and say.

Activities

Prayer on a Shoe

Enlarge and copy the pattern provided as a prayerful morning reminder.

Prayer That Sticks

Make copies of a traditional morning offering either using one of the prayers above or one of your own. Print and cut out four to a page, leaving room for the children to outline the prayer in a color or design of their choice. Once the children have personalized their prayer, make prayer cards by covering each child's prayer with clear contact paper or adhere each card to the corner of each student's desk by covering the card with a slightly larger piece of clear contact paper. This is a great way to reinforce any prayer that you want the children to learn.

Help me God be kind and true
And all my life to follow you.

The Everyday

Aspirations
Short prayers called aspirations help us to stop from giving in to discouragement and frustration such as, "Blessed be God" or "Lord have mercy."

Bedtime Prayer
An important time-honored custom is for Catholics to end the day with a prayer of their choice including praying for special intentions and protection for the night. You may want to send one of the following home or invite the class to share the bedtime prayers they have used at home.

While making the sign of the cross say,

Bless me, God, as this day ends,
Bless my family and all my friends,
Keep me safe through the night,
and wake me with the morning's light.

As I lay my head to sleep,
Good thoughts from this day I will keep.
Be with me until the morning light,
when I will wake to a new day's light.

When I am tucked into my bed,
I close my eyes and rest my head.
And thank you Lord in heaven above.
For covering me with your love.

Activities
Bedtime Pattern
Enlarge and copy the pattern provided as prayerful reminders.

Pillowcase Prayers
All you need to encourage morning and bedtime prayer is a pre-washed, light-colored pillowcase and permanent or fabric markers. Place a large brown grocery bag or square of cardboard in between the fabric of the pillowcase. With adult help, have the children print a morning prayer on one side of the case and a bedtime prayer on the other. Have the children add their names and drawings to the cases and again allow to dry with the grocery bag liner inside.

Daily Prayer Nuts and Bolts
As Catholics we are encouraged to offer daily prayers of adoration, thanksgiving, contrition, and petitions for others and ourselves. Help the children remember to include all of these by inviting them to hold up clinched fists as you explain and invite them to extend a finger with each line.

Activity: *The Fingers of Prayer*

The thumb is our first finger and its movement directs all of the other fingers. This finger reminds us to tell God, first and foremost, I love you!

Now, extend your second finger.

This is the finger we use to point to people and objects around us. Use this finger to remember to say thank you to God for all of the people and things that you have been blessed with.

Extend your middle finger.

The middle finger is often the longest of all a person's fingers. This tall finger reminds us that there are many people who need our prayers. It reminds us to pray for all of those people who need God's help.

Extend your fourth or ring finger.

People often wear rings on this finger that symbolize lifetime commitments. The circle of a ring symbolizes unending or eternal love. The ring finger reminds us to be mindful of God's eternal love and forgiveness for us—remembering the things that need to be forgiven in our lives.

Last but not least, extend your fifth or pinkie finger.

This small finger reminds us of the last building block of our daily prayer, our own requests.

Prayers of Thanksgiving

If we open our eyes and hearts to God's presence, we also find a thankful heart. Traditionally Catholics give thanks to God frequently for blessings such as food and shelter, family and friends, and all the other good things of each day. Teaching children to do this helps to overcome the spirit of grumbling with a spirit of gratitude. Stop what you are doing with the children for just a minute or two to count those blessings. The difference it will make in everyone's day may surprise you!

Activity: *Blessings Five*

Invite each child to point to each finger on one hand as you all count out loud five blessings of the day. The children will be delighted as they hear this melody of blessings offered up with thanksgiving.

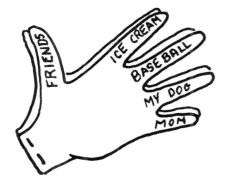

Trace the children's hands on construction paper. Cut them out and staple them together at the wrists. Ask the child to tell you what he or she is thankful for and print one thing on each finger.

Love in Action

Throughout Scripture, we are told of God's awesome, ultimate love for us. This love was shown through the divine gift of his Son, Jesus Christ. Our belief in God, the Spirit and Jesus help us to put love into action. When you give friends a high five, when you clean your room, when you help others, when you pay attention at school … you are praying through your work.

The Everyday

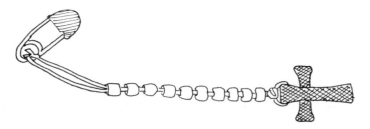

Activity: *Good-Deed Beads*
Gather the following for each child.
1 yard of cord or string
10 pony beads
1 inexpensive cross or medal
1 safety pin

See the diagram for help on stringing the beads. First, string the cross onto the cord and move it to the center. Tie an overhand knot in the cord and pull it tight to the top of the cross. String the beads, one at a time, by running both ends of the cord through the hole from the opposite side. As you add each bead, move it down close to the previous bead to keep the two ends of the cord even. When all beads are strung, hold the two ends of the cord together evenly and tie a knot, leaving a space of about 2 inches from the last bead so you can move the beads up and down. Tie the ends of the cord to the hole at the end of a safety pin. Trim the ends.

Pin the beads to the children's clothes or their backpacks. Each time they do something nice for someone or say a little prayer, they can slip a bead up the string.

Blessings

In Scripture, blessings express God's generosity, favor, and unshakable love for His children.

During the traditional ritual, the right hand is raised and usually the Sign of the Cross is made over the person or thing, invoking God's favor or intervention upon the one blessed.

Many teachers and parents bless the children as they leave for the day, go on a vacation or celebrate an event such as a birthday.

Activities
Jesus Booklet
Use the following story on page 13 to teach the children about Jesus and how much He loves children. Then make the attached booklet to reinforce their understanding.

Hands-on Blessing
Choose from the following gestures and phrases:

May God bless you and keep you.
Go with peace.
        Make a small cross on each child's forehead.

May God bless you and bring you back
 rested and well.
        Give each child a high five.

God be with you!
        Exchange a fist over fist with each child.

You might even sprinkle a bit of glitter in their shoes, tie a colored ribbon to their belt or around their wrist, stamp a heart print on the top of their hand or the bottom of their shoe or give them a little spritz of water to remind them of God's blessing and presence with them.

6

Jesus loved the children of long ago. And he loves children today.

7

Jesus loves me! Amen.

2

Some mothers and children came to see Jesus.

5

But Jesus said, "Let the little children come to me." Then he blessed them.

1

One day, Jesus was very tired from his work. His friends wanted him to rest.

4

His friends called to the mothers, "Take the children away! Jesus is too tired to see them."

Jesus and the Children

3

"Please bless our children," the mothers asked Jesus.

Create a storybook based on Matthew 19:13-15, for the children. Help the children cut the pages on the dotted lines and assemble the booklet in order. Have them color the pictures. Then staple the booklets for them.

The Everyday

Birthday Blessing
Sung to the tune of Happy Birthday.

"May the Dear Lord Bless you!
May the Dear Lord Bless you!
May the Dear Lord Bless ____,
May the Dear Lord Bless you!"

Classroom Blessing
Lord,
We ask you to bless this class.
Let your light shine on us and guide our work,
Always being a reflection of your presence to one another.

A Blessing for the Teacher
Oh Lord, we ask you to bless (teacher's name).
Give her a kind ear to hear us,
the patience to correct us,
and the energy to teach us.
Give her humor to get through the day and
the wisdom to see the gifts each of us brings.

Guardian Angel Prayer

Our Catholic Faith teaches us that God created angels that are special helpers in the world. Psalm 91:11 tells us that God assigns angels to guard people in all that they do. By assigning guardian angels to guide and watch over us, God is demonstrating love and concern for us.

Angel of God, my guardian dear,
To whom God's love commits me here;
Ever this day be at my side
To light and guard, to rule and guide.
Amen.

Activities
Clip-on Guardian Angels

These delightful angels can be clipped on anything from clothing to backpacks to pillowcases.

Using the pattern provided, trace and cut two angels per child out of heavy paper. With gold or white spray paint, paint a spring clothespin for every child in your class. Have the children glue a bit of Spanish moss to the outside of each angel's head for hair and sprinkle with a little glitter. Decorate the rest of the angel with glitter or foil stars. Be sure that the children only decorate one side of each angel, as the other side will be glued to the flat side of the clothespin. With adult help use clear drying glue or a glue gun to attach the angels to the clothespins. Add simple pipe-cleaner halos.

Coffee-filter Sweet Treat Angels

Place hard candy in the center of a coffee filter and close it with a rubber band. Wrap one end of a gold pipe cleaner around the gathered part and extend the other end up and bend it into a circle for a halo. The wings can be made out of paper or felt. Attach the Guardian Angel Prayer.

Glory and Praise Prayer

This prayer refers to the mystery of the three Persons in one God, the Trinity.

Glory be to the Father,
And to the Son,
And to the Holy Spirit.
As it was in the beginning,
Is now, and ever shall be,
World without end. Amen.

Activity: Trinity Shamrock

This is a difficult concept even for adults to grasp. Begin by teaching the Sign of the Cross. Then use the traditional symbols of the Trinity such as the triangle and shamrock in an art project to talk about the three Persons in one God.

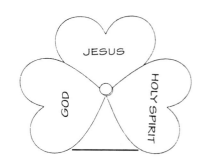

Each child will need three heart shapes and one triangle cut out of green fun foam. Older children can cut their own. Punch a hole through the point of each heart and through the point of the triangle. Use a brad to hold all of the pieces together, making a shamrock. On each heart, write one of the following: God, Jesus and Holy Spirit. The three parts can be separated or stacked on one another to symbolize one God.

The Lord's Prayer

Remind the children that Jesus prayed often. Jesus wants us to pray and He gave us this special prayer to teach us how to pray.

Our Father, who art in heaven, hallowed be your name, your kingdom come, your will be done, on earth as it is in heaven. Give us this day our daily bread and forgive us our trespasses, as we forgive those who trespass against us. And lead us not into temptation, but deliver us from evil. Amen.

The Everyday

Activities
Phrase-by-Phrase
Say the prayer very slowly. Remind the children that this is a very important prayer, because this is the way that Jesus taught us to pray. Ask the following:

What did Jesus mean … (phrase by phrase)?

Hand Prayer Books
Make hand prayer books to emphasize the importance of this prayer.

Fold a large sheet of construction paper—accordion fashion—to create four folds, five sections. Trace the child's hand, with fingers held closely together, on only the first section of the paper. Cut around the outline, being sure to leave some of the folded ends of the hands uncut on each side. Carefully open the paper and glue a copy of the Our Father in the center of the praying hands.

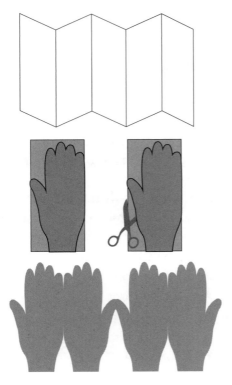

Hail Mary
Catholics are devoted to Mary because she is the Mother of God and our Mother as well. When we pray to Mary, we ask her to pray to God for us.

Hail Mary, full of grace, the Lord is with you. Blessed are you among women and blessed is the fruit of your womb, Jesus. Holy Mary, Mother of God, pray for us sinners, now and at the hour of our death. Amen.

Activities
Statue of Mary
As you are teaching the children this prayer, place a statue of Mary in the room. Talk about some of the wonderful events of Mary's life such as Gabriel's greeting to Mary and the birth of Jesus.

Mary's Feasts
Remind the children that there are many feasts honoring Mary under a variety of titles such as:

Mary, Mother of God, January 1
Birthday of Mary, September 8
The Visitation of Mary, May 31

Traditional Catholic Grace

For centuries, Catholics have offered a prayer of gratitude before their meals. This is the one most commonly known and used.

Bless us, O Lord, and these your gifts, which we are about to receive from your bounty. Through Christ, our Lord. Amen.

Activity: *Grace Mobile*

Make a place-setting mobile to send the message home.

Provide a metal or plastic hanger for each child in your group. Make a copy of the Catholic Grace and have the children glue it to a colored paper plate. Punch a hole in the top of the plate and lace a ribbon through it. Tie the end of the ribbon to the center of the hanger. Punch a hole in a paper napkin and paper cup, attach ribbon and hang them from the hanger. Tie the ribbon to a plastic spoon and fork and hang them also. Adjust the ribbon lengths and space the items so that they look like a hanging table setting.

Intercessory Prayer

Many Catholics traditionally say a quick prayer for everyone they see in need, whether known or strangers. Catholics often make it a habit to go through a mental or written list of people and ask God to bless each one.

Activity: *Prayer Journal*

A large number of Catholics keep a prayer journal as a way of keeping track of those they are praying for. The journal is also a way of deepening their relationship with God.

Journal entries can be put in the form of an address to God, as in:

Dear Jesus,

Today I helped a friend.

I am mad at Dave and I don't get math. Help.

Younger children can reflect their prayers by drawing, coloring and painting as a precursor of a prayer journal. Or, the journal can simply be used to list people you are praying for and things you are praying about.

Begin by giving the children two sheets of construction paper and several sheets of plain white paper for younger children and ruled paper for older children. Invite the children to print the words "Prayer Journal" and then decorate the covers, both front and back. Leave some of the inside pages blank and include some traditional Catholic prayers on other pages.

Meditative Prayer

Meditation means reflecting or reading about some truth of our faith, often pausing to lift your heart to God. It is a Catholic custom to spend some time each day on meditation.

For example: Read a passage slowly and reflectively and receive it as a personal message from God. Awareness of God speaking to us is an important aspect of spiritual development.

Realize that the ability to hear this inner voice requires a life that regularly has quiet and peaceful times. Many religions include times of silence as part of prayer. It's important that adults provide quiet times and spaces for children.

Activity: *Picturing Scripture*

Painting or drawing has an amazing ability to calm, to slow down thought and to help us focus on the moment. Read a short story from Scripture. Then ask the children to draw or paint something about the story while you read it to them again. Read the Scripture story one more time and then let the children finish their drawings or paintings. Conclude with a showing of pictures, and allow each child to share their special interpretation.

The Jesus Prayer

This prayer consists of prayerfully repeating the name of Jesus over and over again.

Activity: *Images of Jesus*

Place a physical image of Christ in a place the children will see frequently. Show the children portraits from modern times as well as century old renditions. Some show Christ in a very serious light, others smiling, even laughing. You can look at the infant Jesus, Christ crucified, Jesus with children, etc. Looking at all of these images with the children is a prayer in itself.

Eventually the Jesus prayer can become part of the rhythm of one's breathing and enter into the heart in a way that is truly sanctifying.

Sacramentals

In popular thinking, sacramentals are often equated with blessed objects used for a religious purpose. But are they always objects?

Sacramentals are sacred signs, both objects and actions, that reflect the truths of our Faith. They include religious signs, symbols, public and private devotions, prayers, gestures, rituals, music, images, and natural or manmade objects. Some of them are found only in the church's official rituals such as sacred oils. Others are common to daily life, such as candles and holy water. In themselves they might not be religious but they become sacramentals and holy in their purpose and use. This section will explore the more common Catholic sacramentals that touch our daily lives.

The Rosary

The rosary is a traditional prayer to honor Mary. Rosary means, "garland of roses." It is a garland of prayer to Mary. According to Tradition, Mary revealed this prayer to St. Dominic and offered it as a way for Catholics to ponder in their hearts the mysteries of the life of Jesus in an easy-to-understand form. The rosary recalls the principal mysteries of our salvation in groups of five decades and is preceded by the recitation of the Creed, and three Hail Mary's for an increase in faith, hope, and charity.

Prayer Books

Many Catholics use prayer books everyday to inspire their prayer. Continue to nourish the prayer lives of the children by collecting several of the prayers you have shared and putting them into prayer books made by the children.

Activities
Prayers on a Ring

Mount the prayers on index cards and have the children add a design element to each. Cover both sides of the index card with clear packaging tape or have them laminated at a copy shop. Punch a hole in the upper left corner of each card. Insert a clip key ring to make a flip-the-page prayer book.

Prayer Book

Make copies of the children's prayer book pattern on page 21.

Cross and Crucifix

No Christian symbol is more common or speaks more clearly than the Cross. It recalls the fundamental belief of Christianity giving us a powerful sign of God's victory and undying love for us.

Catholic crosses often include the body of the crucified Christ on them as a remembrance that Jesus died for our sins and a way of showing that He is the center of our lives. The crucifixion is a difficult topic for young children. Don't dwell on the death of Christ; always mention Jesus' rising in conjunction with His death.

Activity: *Cross Bookmarks*

Cut out an 8-inch cross from construction paper. Cut four horizontal slits on the cross.

Have the children weave 10-inch ribbons through the slits.

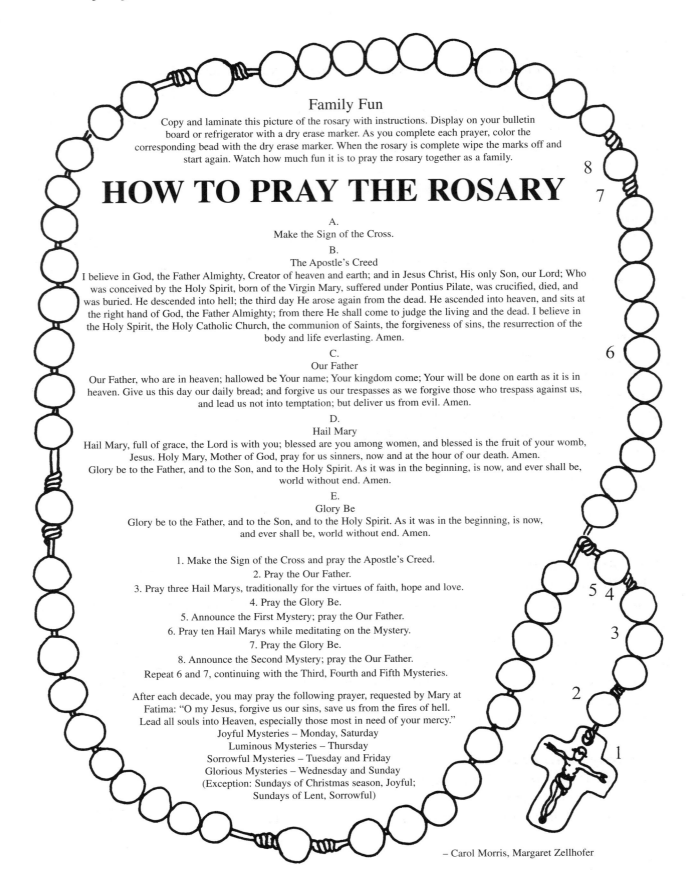

Family Fun
Copy and laminate this picture of the rosary with instructions. Display on your bulletin board or refrigerator with a dry erase marker. As you complete each prayer, color the corresponding bead with the dry erase marker. When the rosary is complete wipe the marks off and start again. Watch how much fun it is to pray the rosary together as a family.

HOW TO PRAY THE ROSARY

A.
Make the Sign of the Cross.

B.
The Apostle's Creed
I believe in God, the Father Almighty, Creator of heaven and earth; and in Jesus Christ, His only Son, our Lord; Who was conceived by the Holy Spirit, born of the Virgin Mary, suffered under Pontius Pilate, was crucified, died, and was buried. He descended into hell; the third day He arose again from the dead. He ascended into heaven, and sits at the right hand of God, the Father Almighty; from there He shall come to judge the living and the dead. I believe in the Holy Spirit, the Holy Catholic Church, the communion of Saints, the forgiveness of sins, the resurrection of the body and life everlasting. Amen.

C.
Our Father
Our Father, who are in heaven; hallowed be Your name; Your kingdom come; Your will be done on earth as it is in heaven. Give us this day our daily bread; and forgive us our trespasses as we forgive those who trespass against us, and lead us not into temptation; but deliver us from evil. Amen.

D.
Hail Mary
Hail Mary, full of grace, the Lord is with you; blessed are you among women, and blessed is the fruit of your womb, Jesus. Holy Mary, Mother of God, pray for us sinners, now and at the hour of our death. Amen.
Glory be to the Father, and to the Son, and to the Holy Spirit. As it was in the beginning, is now, and ever shall be, world without end. Amen.

E.
Glory Be
Glory be to the Father, and to the Son, and to the Holy Spirit. As it was in the beginning, is now, and ever shall be, world without end. Amen.

1. Make the Sign of the Cross and pray the Apostle's Creed.
2. Pray the Our Father.
3. Pray three Hail Marys, traditionally for the virtues of faith, hope and love.
4. Pray the Glory Be.
5. Announce the First Mystery; pray the Our Father.
6. Pray ten Hail Marys while meditating on the Mystery.
7. Pray the Glory Be.
8. Announce the Second Mystery; pray the Our Father.
Repeat 6 and 7, continuing with the Third, Fourth and Fifth Mysteries.

After each decade, you may pray the following prayer, requested by Mary at Fatima: "O my Jesus, forgive us our sins, save us from the fires of hell. Lead all souls into Heaven, especially those most in need of your mercy."
Joyful Mysteries – Monday, Saturday
Luminous Mysteries – Thursday
Sorrowful Mysteries – Tuesday and Friday
Glorious Mysteries – Wednesday and Sunday
(Exception: Sundays of Christmas season, Joyful;
Sundays of Lent, Sorrowful)

– Carol Morris, Margaret Zellhofer

Night:

I have lived and loved and laughed today. Now I must rest until tomorrow. Thank you for this day and good night, Jesus! Amen.

Morning:

Good morning, Jesus! Thank you for time to sleep and time to wake. Watch over me in this new day. Amen.

Meal:

Jesus, you shared bread with your friends. Thank you for the tastes, smells, and colors of the foods I have today. Amen.

Play:

Dear Jesus, now it is time to play so I can learn about our world. Thank you for my imagination! Amen.

Directions to make a prayer book for class: Copy this page for each child. Invite the children to add pages with their own pictures and prayers. Cut on lines. Make a construction-paper cover. Title the book "_____'s Book of Prayer." Help each child print their name in space and decorate cover.

Candles

The use of holy candles is a visible and prominent Catholic custom. Candles symbolize Jesus as the Light of the world. Jesus describes himself as light: "I am the light of the world. No follower of mine shall ever walk in darkness" (John 8:12).

Since ancient times, light has reminded people of God's presence, joy, happiness, goodness, purity, and life. Catholics often light candles in church as an outward symbol of prayers offered.

Two kinds of burning lights, so evident in most Catholic churches and shrines, are the votive candle and vigil lights. The votive candle is associated with seeking some favor from the Lord or a saint. The vigil candle indicates a prayer of attention or waiting.

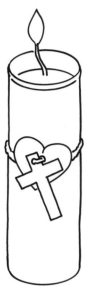

Activity: *Votive Decorations*

Purchase votive candles that come in a plastic liner for each child. Make copies of the cross and heart patterns. Have each child cut out a heart and a cross. Use a paper-punch to make a hole, lace ribbon through them for tying to the side of the candle.

Holy Water

Another popular religious tradition is the use of holy water. It is used to bless oneself, others and objects. Every Catholic Church has holy water fonts near its entrance where visitors can bless themselves as they enter the church. The usual practice is to dip one's fingers into the water and to make the sign of the cross: "In the name of the Father, and of the Son, and of the Holy Spirit." Taking holy water as you enter the church is a way of remembering that you have been baptized into the life, death and resurrection of Christ.

Activities
Classroom Font

Put a small holy water font by the entrance to your room. The font is kept full of holy water, which can be obtained at church by asking the priest or by drawing the water from the special container for that purpose. Simple water fonts can be obtained at most Catholic religious goods stores.

Take-Home Fonts

Often Catholic families keep a small amount of holy water in their homes.

Collect small glass jars and have the children decorate the jars with paints. Print labels with "Holy Water" on them. Once the paint has dried, carefully label each jar.

Take the children down to the church and explain what makes this water special and holy. Give each child a small amount of holy water to take home. Encourage the children to use the water to bless the members of their family.

Icons

It is a universal custom in the Eastern rites of the Catholic Church to display icons in churches and homes. Icons differ from Western art works on the same themes in that they are supposed to be painted only by those who pray deeply about their work; the painting therefore becomes a fruit of contemplation. Icons help us to feel connected to our church communities and to remind us of Jesus' presence in our lives.

Icons are often found in the entryways of some houses and may be rotated according to the feast days that have just been celebrated.

Activity: *Icon Show-and-Tell*

Many Catholics collect icons. Invite someone from your parish to come in and talk about the meaning and significance of their favorite icons. Show the children pictures or samples of other religious art.

Then give the children the opportunity to prayerfully create a piece of their own religious art.

John the Baptist

Holy Cards

Catholics often carry this concrete reminder of their faith with them.

Activity: *Making Holy Cards*

Make holy cards by typing a prayer into a computer that has a greeting-card program. This allows you to create a decorative holy card. Print the holy cards out on cardstock quality paper. You can add a picture to the side opposite of the prayer or have the children draw a picture that relates to the prayer. The cards can be covered with clear contact paper.

Bells

Bells were used to call people to Mass, to prayer and to gather people for important parish news.

Activity: *Prayer Bells*

Have the children decorate the outside of a 3" flower pot with paints or stickers. Allow to dry. Make handles by cutting twine in 24" lengths. Pull the twine through a 1/2" bead or jingle bell and fold in half so that the bead is at the folded end of twine. Make a double knot 3" above the bead and pull the ends of the twine through the bottom of the bell making sure the knot is secure and does not go through the hole. Make a new double knot on the top of the bell, again making sure the knot holds the twine in place. To make a loop for hanging, tie a knot with the ends of the twine. Use a bell to call the children to prayer and encourage the children to take their bells home to do the same.

Medals

The wearing of religious medals is a common Catholic tradition. These medals serve as a reminder of personal faith and religious commitment. There are many kinds of holy medals that Catholics traditionally wear around their necks, on bracelets, keep in their pockets or purses as a sign of devotion or as a petition for intercession and protection.

Activity: *Juice-Can-Lid Medals*

Make simple juice-can-lid medals to tie to backpacks, belt loops, or to each child's desk.

Use a nail and hammer to punch a hole through a juice-can lid. Be sure to hammer down any rough places the nail may have caused on the backside of the lid. Place a sticker of Jesus on one side of the lid and a picture of the child, or simply the child's name with a permanent marker. Thread a piece of cording or leather through the hole and tie the lid to the child's backpack or belt loop. Remind the children that Jesus walks with us every minute of every day.

The Missal

It is a custom for Catholics to read and meditate on the Scripture passages for the upcoming Mass. The Missal is available as either a large single volume or several smaller volumes providing the readings for Masses throughout the year.

Activity: *Getting to Know the Missal*

Keep a Missal in your room and show the children how it is used. Get the children in the habit of reading and thinking about the Scriptures for the upcoming Mass ahead of time. Use a Children's Lectionary each week to briefly go over the upcoming readings. After each reading, ask the children a related question to get them thinking about the meaning of the reading.

Novena

Novena comes from the Latin word for nine and refers to nine days of prayer. It has been a tradition in the church for several centuries to pray to a particular saint, to Mary, or to Jesus, for a special intention for nine consecutive days, repeating the same prayer nine times. Have you ever seen a thank you to St. Jude, the patron saint of hopeless cases, posted in the newspaper? Many

Catholics believe that when you make a novena to St. Jude you are to thank the saint publicly when your prayer is answered. An example of an old traditional novena is to the child Jesus. One would kneel before an image of the child Jesus and pray the "Glory Be" twelve times, with hands cupped open to receive the many blessings God showered down on you.

Activity: *Praying-Hands Novena*

When the children are aware of someone with a very special need such as someone having surgery or someone who is ill, lead them or encourage them to pray for nine consecutive days.

Help them remember what a novena is by having each child trace their hands on colored construction paper and cut them out. On the inside of each hand, print the intention. Inset a brad at the wrists of each set of hands, so that when opened at the fingers, the intention is revealed. Then cut 9 paper strips to make links for a chain. Each day for nine consecutive days of prayer, add a paper link to the chain until you have added all nine.

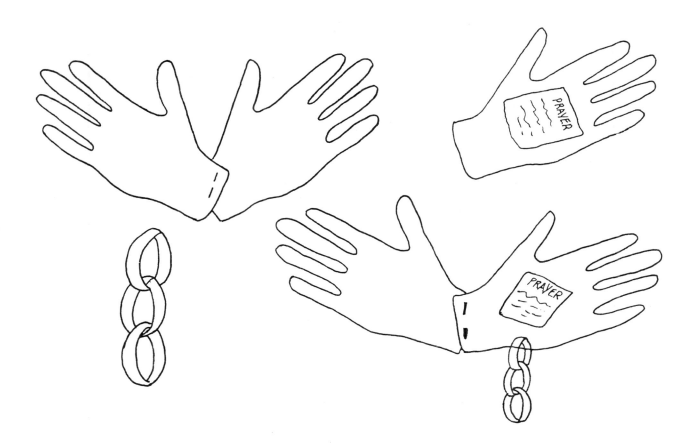

Project Checklist

_____
_____
_____
_____
_____
_____
_____
_____
_____
_____
_____
_____
_____
_____
_____
_____
_____
_____
_____
_____
_____
_____

September at a Glance

Dedication for September: The Seven Sorrows

September's Liturgical Color

Patron Saints of the Month

September Stories of Welcome!

First Sunday in September: Labor Day

September 8: The Birthday of Mary

September 9: St. Peter Claver

September 14: Feast of the Holy Cross

September 20: Sts. Andrew Kim Taegon, Paul Chong Hasang and Companions

September 21: St. Matthew

September 22: First Day of Autumn and Celebration Table Ideas

September 23: Autumn Equinox

September 25: St. Sergius of Radnonezh

September 27: St. Vincent de Paul

September 29: Feast of the Archangels or Michaelmas

Dedication for September: The Seven Sorrows

This dedication recognizes the sadness experienced by Mary, the devoted mother of Jesus. September 15 is called "Our Lady of Sorrows" day.

The Seven Sorrows are:

1. Prophecy of Simeon
2. Flight into Egypt
3. Lost in the Temple
4. Meeting on the Way of the Cross
5. Crucifixion
6. Taking down from the Cross
7. Burial

September's Liturgical Color

Ordinary Time: Green

Green is the color of hope and life.

Patron Saints of the Month

September 21: Matthew: accountants, bankers, bookkeepers, tax collectors

September

September Stories of Welcome!

The beginning of the school year may find children a little uneasy or shy, but it also offers them an opportunity to learn to welcome others. Here are two stories about welcoming the newcomer. The first is an Old Testament story of Abraham's hospitality, and the second echoes the same story in a modern setting. Read both with the children and enjoy the follow-up activities.

Welcome Friends: Abraham's Guests

Abraham was sitting by his tent, which was his home. It was very hot. He noticed three men standing under the nearby oak trees. Abraham jumped up and ran to them. Abraham bowed to the ground in front of them to show them he was friendly and respectful. "You are welcome here! Please stay and rest," he said as he stood up. "You must be hot and tired. I will bring you water to wash your feet. Rest in the shade of these trees, I will be back with food, too!"

Abraham hurried to the tent where he asked his wife, Sarah, to make bread, using only their best flour. He chose the most tender meat to be cooked. Abraham then went to get milk and cheese. As soon as the food was all ready, he brought everything before the guests. He stood near them while they ate.

Abraham did not know it then, but his guests were angels!

Discussion Starter: How did Abraham welcome his guests? Who were his guests?

Welcome Friends: Zach's Guest

It was the first day of school. Zach sat down on the rug with the other children. The teacher said, "Welcome! I hope you will enjoy being in my class! Let's start with a story."

As the teacher read, Zach looked around. He thought he liked school, but he felt a bit afraid. He wished just a little that he was at home, playing with his toys right now. The teacher seemed nice, but he'd rather have been with his dad instead.

Just as the story was finished, there was a knock at the door, and the teacher went to answer it. When she came back to the rug, she was leading a little girl by the hand. The girl looked very shy, even a bit afraid.

"Children, this is Mikiko. She just moved here from Japan and doesn't speak English yet. Because no one here speaks her language, we will have to show her that she is welcome. Zach, would you find Mikiko a place to sit for snack?"

Zach looked at Mikiko's scared face. He forgot he wished he were home. He smiled at her. Then he took Mikiko's hand and led her to a table. He patted a chair so Mikiko knew she should sit down, and he sat next to her. He pointed to her juice cup and cracker, rubbed his tummy and smiled. Mikiko smiled and rubbed her tummy too. Soon, Zach and Mikiko were eating and giggling together.

"Thank you, Zach, for helping Mikiko feel welcome already," the teacher said.

Discussion Starter: How did Zach help Mikiko feel welcome? Who was Mikiko?

Activities
Welcoming Rituals
After reading the stories, tell the children that Jesus always welcomes children (see Luke 18:15-16). Then call each child forward, one by one, saying, "Jesus welcomes [name]." Then encourage the others to chorus, "And so do we!"

Place Mats
Make place mats to extend the welcome theme. Give each child a large piece of colorful construction paper on which you have written 'WELCOME!' Each child then draws something on it, and passes it to his/her right. Then they each draw something on the next one. Each place mat will have a drawing done by all class members. Cover the mats with clear contact paper. These can be used at snack time for the first few weeks.

Meal Prayer
At snack or lunchtime, add this to your prayer: "Please help us make our classroom a welcoming place, as Abraham welcomed his guests. Amen."

First Sunday in September – Labor Day
"For we are God's fellow workers; you are God's field, God's building."
    1 Corinthians 3: 9
"... whatever you do, do all to the glory of God."
    1 Corinthians 10: 31

Prayer
Today we give thanks for the gift of work. We may not always like it, but the responsibilities and jobs we have at home and school will help us grow up to be capable and happy people. We are grateful for our parents and teachers who show us how to take care of ourselves, our homes, and schools and who model the value of work. As we grow older we pray that we will continue to learn how to do many new things that will benefit others and ourselves. Help us to remember

September

to give glory to God in everything we do each day, through our work and play. Amen.

History

Labor Day is a legal holiday celebrated on the first Monday of September. It honors all those who work. The three-day Labor Day weekend has come to mark the end of summer and the beginning of fall. Many communities begin school the Tuesday after this holiday weekend.

Labor Day came into being after the Industrial Revolution. Workers were not happy with the harsh working conditions and long hours they were expected to work. At this time there were no rules to protect adults and children from dangerous working conditions and long weeks of work. Labor unions, groups of people who organized themselves to work for safer conditions and shorter workdays and weeks were formed to change this. In time labor unions were successful and eventually the first Labor Day was celebrated in 1882 with a parade in New York City. In 1887 Oregon was the first state to recognize Labor Day as a legal holiday. President Grover Cleveland made Labor Day a federal holiday in 1894. As Catholics, we can be proud of our Church's history on labor. The rights and welfare of workers was a large concern amongst Catholics of the 19th century. In 1891, Pope Leo XIII issued the encyclical Rerum Novarum, which extensively focused on labor issues.

Activities
A List to Be Thankful for

Talk about work and why it is important. Ask the children about the jobs they have at home and school and why they are important. Name some of the different jobs that people do in our communities. What jobs do people have that keep us safe or provide us with the things we need each day? Make a list together and display it in your classroom. Remind the children that we are thankful for the work of many people. What would we do without the work of the farmer, doctor, teacher, mail carrier, etc? Remind the children that we should be grateful that God gave so many people good minds and creative hands that help make our lives safe and comfortable.

Guessing Professions

Play a guessing game to help the children with their understanding of the different jobs men and women do. Gather an assortment of hats that different workers would wear as they do their jobs. Include hats from fire fighters, police officers, painters, cooks, doctors, construction workers, etc. Put them (one at a time) in a brown bag and give the children clues as to the kinds of things the person who wears this hat would do. The child who makes the first correct guess gets to wear that hat. Display the hats in your room with a sign that reads, "We are thankful for workers who help us."

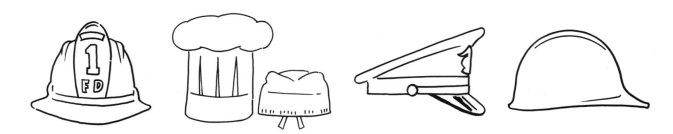

Parent-Talk

Invite parents or other members of your community to come in and talk about their jobs. Ask people how they became interested in their work and why they like it.

Have the children think about and share the kinds of work that they would like to do when they grow up. Make a bulletin board titled, "When I Grow Up..." Have the children draw a self-portrait of what they think they will look like when they grow up and with adult help write on it the kind of work they want to do.

Thank-You Letters

Write letters to the fire fighters, police officers and others who work in your community. Thank them for working hard and being there to help us and keep us safe.

September 8 – The Birthday of Mary

We have no definite record of Mary's birthday. September was chosen by the Eastern churches back in the sixth century. In some parts of Europe, her birthday is combined with harvest blessings and processions.

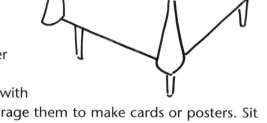

Activity: *A Party for Mary*

Young children are quick to appreciate a birthday. What better way to help them feel close to our Mother than by celebrating her birth?

Provide the children with a statue of Mary, a cake with candles, and perhaps some flowers or balloons. Encourage them to make cards or posters. Sit down together and feast. Talk about Mary and her love for us. Sing "Happy Birthday."

September 9 – St. Peter Claver

Did you ever wonder how slavery got started in our country? It began hundreds of years ago when large numbers of people were kidnapped from African countries and forced to come to the Americas in a ship. They were treated very badly, so many died on the ships. Those who lived were sold as slaves.

Do you wonder if anyone cared about these people? There were people who did, and who worked against slavery. One was Peter Claver, a Spanish priest. He met the ships where they came into the country we call Columbia. He had to convince the ships' captains to let him on board. Peter brought with him gifts of medicine, bandages, and food. He found lawyers to help. He talked with slave owners, fighting for the rights of enslaved people. He spoke with the Africans, telling them that God loved and valued them. He baptized them, performed weddings, and taught them about Christianity. He preached in the city square and to the sailors and slave traders about the dignity of the African people. Peter did this work for 38 years. We celebrate the work and love of Peter Claver on this day.

September 14 – Feast of the Holy Cross

The cross is the most important and recognizable symbol of Christianity. While young children are not ready to fully understand that crucifixion was a death penalty, they are probably well aware of the symbol itself. On this day, display a cross where children can easily see it. Talk about how often we Christians make the Sign of the Cross: when we enter or leave a church, at mealtimes, at bedtime prayers, etc. Tell them that the Sign was part of their baptisms. Make the Sign of the Cross with them. Review what the words mean. Go slowly and reverently. Make sure they understand that their hands trace the shape of the cross.

Activity: *Hand Cross*

To further remind the children of the importance of the cross for each one of them, make a cross with their hands. Trace each child's hand on a piece of construction paper and have the child cut it out. Ask the children to print their names on their hands. Glue the hands to a larger piece of paper in the form of a cross, symbolizing that Christ came to earth to help us live good lives because He loves us so much.

September 20 – Sts. Andrew Kim Taegon, Paul Chong Hasang and Companions

Today there are many Christian people in Korea. Less than 200 years ago, however, Christians were martyred there for their faith. The topic of martyrdom is a difficult one for young children. However, it is important that they realize that saints come from all parts of the world. On this day, tell them that a young man named Andrew Kim Taegon and others so loved Jesus that they were willing to give their lives in order to show others how important Jesus is.

Discussion Starter: How can we show others how important Jesus is to us?

September 21 – St. Matthew

Matthew was not well liked. His job was to collect taxes from people. Now most everyone has to pay taxes, but the Jewish people of Matthew's time resented whom they had to pay. The Romans ran the government, and the Jewish people did not feel it was fair that they had to pay their money to the Romans. Besides this, some tax payers cheated by collecting more money than the law required. We don't know what kind of tax collector Matthew was. We do know that Jesus chose him to be one of His apostles. And Matthew became a great man who taught many others about Jesus. In the gospel of Matthew, many of the stories tell us that Jesus loves people of all kinds.

Activity: *Matthew's Gospel*

Share a couple of the stories from Matthew that reflect Jesus' love for all people such as Matthew 5: 1-12 and Matthew 9: 10-13.

September 22 – First Day of Autumn

The season of Autumn comes between summer and winter. In the United States we also call this season fall probably because of the falling leaves from the trees. In the fall of the year children start back to school after summer vacation and the farmers are working hard to bring in the harvest.

As the season of Autumn draws near,
We see signs of change everywhere.

The leaves change color without a sound
They twirl and float and then fall down.

The birds take flight and all fly south,
They know just where to go and never have doubt.

Apples turn color as they sit on the tree,
They're ready to be picked by you and by me.

The days are shorter and cooler we know it is true,
Summer is gone and winter is due.

Activities

Enjoy the Sights

Take a nature walk and look for the signs of fall. Talk about the birds flying south and the days getting shorter and cooler.

Leaf Art

Rake the leaves in your churchyard into a big pile and take turns jumping in. Make a leave church by raking the leaves into a kind of outline of the floor plan of your church. Say a little prayer in the leaf church when it is completed. Make a leafe cross or other symbols of our faith with the fallen leaves.

Fall Wall Hanging

Make a fall wall hanging with nuts, acorns, pinecones, dried berries, sticks and other items you may find on your nature walk. Give each child a small bag with their name on it to collect their items. Use burlap upholstery strips to make the wall hangings. (Burlap upholstery stripping is heavier than regular burlap and has a finished edge. This material is used underneath chairs and sofas and may be purchased for about $.59 a yard at a fabric store.) Cut the burlap into 8" pieces. With a pencil poke a hole at the top of each side of the burlap about 1" from the edge. Weave a stick through the holes and attach a piece of twine to each end of the stick to make a hanger. Use generous amounts of glue to fasten the found items from the nature walk to the the burlap.

Allow to dry overnight on wax paper. Attach the above poem and send home.

Leaf People

Make leaf people by gluing the leaves to a piece of construction paper and adding a head, arms and legs to the leaf. Use only leaves glued to paper to make animals and other things.

Tape a large leaf or several small ones to a piece of paper.

Place another piece of light colored paper on top of the taped leaves. Rub lightly with the side of a crayon over the paper to make a leaf-rubbing picture.

Before ironing leaves between two pieces of wax paper sprinkle a bit of gold glitter on top of the leaves. Cut around the leaves after they have cooled and tape them to your windows.

Place a candle in the middle of the arrangement and use it on your Celebration Table.

Celebration Table

Collect acorns and pinecones and arrange with leaves in the center of a clay flowerpot saucer.

September 23 – Autumn Equinox

This day marks the official change of seasons. Using a globe or map, help children understand that now, in the Northern Hemisphere, the nights will be longer than the days. This is autumn. The opposite is true for the Southern Hemisphere where spring is beginning.

The full moon closest to the autumn equinox is called the "harvest moon." Long ago, the wonderful light from this moon helped farmers work into the night to harvest crops. This is the perfect time to give thanks for God's awe-inspiring creation!

Activity: Autumn Moon Picture

Make autumn moon pictures with construction paper (dark blue or black) for the sky and (orange) full moon.

September 25 – St. Sergius of Radnonezh
Story: St. Sergius and the Old Man

Long ago, in the wooded country of Russia lived a family with three boys, Peter, Stephen, and Sergius. They had a wealthy life at first, but then fighting broke out among the princes of their land. The family had to flee for safety, leaving behind their home and rich life. The parents became farmers, but the boys were still able to go to school. Peter and Stephen learned fast and well. But Sergius could not learn to read and write. Grown-ups were angry with him and children made fun of him. Sergius was miserable.

One day a horse got lost and Sergius went searching for it. Along the way, he met an old man. Little Sergius looked at him. The man looked like the angels in paintings Sergius had seen.

"What do you want, child?" the man asked gently.

Now Sergius was a rather poor child. There were probably many things he could have asked for, but Sergius said immediately, "More than anything, I want to learn to read and write."

The man gave Sergius a piece of sweet bread, and then offered to come to Sergius' house to pray with his family. At prayer, the man asked Sergius to read from the Bible. And Sergius could! He read clearly and smoothly. As he and his family stared at each other in amazement, the old man disappeared.

Had Sergius been helped by an angel? He certainly could read and write now! And, he became very holy. Sergius grew up to be a large, strong man, who chose to live by himself in a wild, lonely place in a great forest. There he could feel close to God. But later, others heard of his holiness and came to learn from him. He taught them how to pray, and how to farm. He helped hundreds of people come closer to God. Now, seven hundred years later, Sergius is a saint greatly loved by the people of his home, Russia.

Discussion Starter: When did St. Sergius realize that he could read? Who do you think the man was?

September 27 – St. Vincent de Paul

The de Paul family were poor, hard-working people in France. Vincent had five brothers and sisters. Seeing how intelligent Vincent was, his parents sold their much-needed ox so they had enough money to send Vincent to school.

Vincent became a priest. At that time in France, there were extremely rich people and many, many more very poor people. Vincent knew he could have an easy life by working for the rich people. It didn't take him long to see that God was calling him to other work. Vincent began working for the poor and hungry people of his country. He set up places for food to be made and given to anyone who needed it. He found recipes for very nutritious food. He built homes for orphaned children, for people too handicapped or too old to take care of themselves. He turned to his very rich friends for help. He asked them for money and he asked them to work too. Many people, rich and poor, began to do the work Vincent did. Now, more than three hundred years later, there are still people doing Vincent's good work.

Discussion Starter: What can we do to continue the work of St. Vincent?

September 29 – Feast of the Archangels or Michaelmas

The days between today's feast and October 2nd (feast of the Guardian Angels) are known by children as "the angel days."

Angels are signs of God's care and love. They remind us how God knows each of us. When we say the Nicene Creed, we say we believe in one God "maker of all that is seen and unseen." God created the angels, whether we see them or not, and they are most wondrous to contemplate!

September

Take these days to learn about angels and celebrate them in a variety of ways:

The Archangels: There are nine classes of angels, as listed in Colossians 1:16, and Romans 8:38. Archangels are one of these. Names of three are given in the Bible—Michael, Gabriel, and Raphael—and they are the ones celebrated on this feast day. There are others who are named in traditional sources and from Jewish books: Uriel, Jophiel, Chamael, Zadkiel, and Jophkiel.

Here are descriptions of the three biblical archangels. Use them to introduce children to them.

The Archangel Gabriel: The word angel means "messenger" and Gabriel is the archangel who brought very important messages from God. We learn of him in the Old Testament book of Daniel. In the New Testament, Gabriel came to Zechariah to tell him of the child, John the Baptist, that Zechariah and Elizabeth would have. And, of course, it was Gabriel who came to Mary, asking her to be the Mother of God. Tradition has it that Gabriel will sound the trumpet on the day of judgment, calling all people from all times and places. Gabriel has been pictured in many examples of fine religious art. The name means "God is my strength."

The Archangel Raphael: Raphael appears only in one book of the Bible, the Book of Tobit. This is a wonderful story of guidance, healing and love. (See below.) However, in the Gospel of John, in the story about the healing pool where Jesus heals a man, tradition says it was Raphael who stirred those waters.

Story: Traveling with an Angel

(Based on the Book of Tobit.)

Long ago there lived a man named Tobit, his wife Anna, and their son, Tobias. They were good people who loved God. Tobit had become blind and was now very unhappy. He even prayed to die, and one day called Tobias to him.

"My son, when I am gone, always honor your mother. Pray each day and keep God's laws. Give to those who are in need, and marry a Jewish girl," the father said. "Now I must tell you that long ago, I left money with my cousin Raguel. It's time to get it back. Find someone to travel with you. It's a long way."

Tobias met a pleasant traveler named Raphael. Along the way, near a river, a fish bit Tobias. "Catch it!" Raphael shouted. He did. They ate part of it, but Raphael decided they should keep the rest to make medicines. Then he said, "Your relative has a daughter named Sarah. You should marry her."

Tobias' eyes grew wide. "I've heard about Sarah. She has gotten married seven times, but all her husbands died right after the wedding! They say there is a demon who kills them!"

"Leave the demon to me," Raphael said mysteriously. "Sarah is smart, brave, and beautiful. God wants you to marry her."

At Raguel's home, Tobias met Sarah. Raphael told Tobias to take part of the fish and put it on the fire, then pray with Sarah. The demon ran away! Tobias and Sarah got married.

Sarah's parents blessed them. Raguel gave Tobias his father's money, and the newlyweds started for Tobias' home with Raphael. When they came near, Raphael took out the last of the fish. "Tobias, when you first see your father, rub this on his eyes. He will see again."

Sad Tobit was sitting quietly, hoping his son would return. Tobias ran up, calling, "Let me help you!" He rubbed the fish onto his father's eyes.

"I can see! Praise God! I can see! Praise the angels!" Tobit shouted. "And you have brought me a daughter-in-law! God has blessed us! Thank you, God!" He did a little dance with Sarah.

Breathless from shouting and dancing, Tobit said, "Tobias, take half the money Raguel gave you and give it to Raphael."

"No," Raphael said. "Instead, thank God. Never stop praising God. Do good, pray, and give to others. I am Raphael, one of God's angels."

The family grabbed each other's hands, afraid now.

"Don't be afraid," Raphael said. "God sent me to you. But now, I must go back to God."

So the great angel went back to God, and Tobit, who no longer wanted to die, lived many more years. He did everything that Raphael said. And he played with his seven grandsons. No doubt he told them stories of the angel named Raphael.

The Archangel Michael: In the Old Testament, Michael is described as standing guard over God's people. The Book of Revelation tells how Michael cast the angels out of heaven who thought they were like God. Michael's name means, "Who is like God?" Michael is thought of as a great protector, and is often shown by artists as dressed in armor, fighting Lucifer, the head of the "fallen" angels. Sometimes the evil one is depicted as a dragon.

Because Michael fights against evil, his feast day offers images of good versus evil. As young as they are, children have an intuitive understanding of this. You need not point out evil in the world to them. They will easily identify with Michael's strength and he offers them a much better model than a television superhero!

Activity: *Like Michael*

Allow some outside play in which they can pretend to be as strong as St. Michael. Fairly harmless "swords" can be made with rolled-up newspaper. Knight each child, and send them off to do good in the world.

In some countries, September 29th is known as Michaelmas, and has been celebrated since the Middle Ages. Many traditions have sprung up around it, and harvest themes are incorporated. Some countries have certain foods for this day. One is Michaelmas rolls, which could easily become a custom at home or in the classroom. In keeping with the dragon theme, you can form a dragon shape out of bread dough, making sure it has a long tail. Scales can be made with small bits of dough pressed into the side, and dried fruits to create eyes and teeth. Dragon bread will be a fearsome feast!

Project Checklist

_____
_____
_____
_____
_____
_____
_____
_____
_____
_____
_____
_____
_____
_____
_____
_____
_____
_____
_____
_____

October at a Glance

Dedication for October: The Holy Rosary
October's Liturgical Color
Patron Saints of the Month
October 1: St. Thérèse of the Child Jesus
October 2: Feast of the Guardian Angels
October 4: St. Francis of Assisi
Harvest Story and Celebration Table Ideas
Sukkot, the Jewish Harvest Celebration
October 18: St. Luke
October 28: Sts. Simon and Jude
October 31: All Hallows' Eve

Dedication for October: The Holy Rosary

October 7 is the feast of Our Lady of the Rosary. During this month traditionally dedicated to Mary, say a decade of the rosary with children as often as possible. With this, introduce them to the five Joyful Mysteries: the Annunciation, the Visitation, the Nativity, the Presentation, and the Finding of Jesus in the Temple.

October's Liturgical Color

Ordinary Time: Green
Green is color of hope and life.

Patron Saints of the Month

October 1: Thérèse of the Child Jesus (the Little Flower): aviators, florists, missionaries
October 4: Francis of Assisi: ecologists, Italy, merchants
October 15: Teresa of Avila: Spain, people with headaches
October 16: Hedwig of Poland: duchesses and queens, young brides, widows

October 1 – St. Thérèse of the Child Jesus

A little more than one hundred years ago in France there lived a little girl named Thérèse Martin. She was full of mischief and loved to play tricks on her four big sisters. But when Thérèse did not get her way, she would kick and scream until she was so tired, she couldn't scream anymore! One thing she loved to do was to hang onto an arm of a chair and swing on it. Grown-ups and big sisters warned her not to do this, but stubborn Thérèse did it anyway. One day, the chair toppled over and Thérèse landed— not on the floor, but in a bucket of scrub water, and she was stuck!

But Thérèse was also a child who loved Jesus very much. She prayed and thought about God often. She became very holy, and is now a saint thousands of people love. There is even a nickname for St. Thérèse—the Little Flower.

Discussion Starter: What kinds of things did St. Thérèse do?

October 2 – The Guardian Angels

We continue the angel day's celebration by honoring our guardian angels this day. Our belief in each person having a special protector who is a gift from God, comes from Jesus' words, "Take care that you do not despise one of these little ones for, I tell you, in heaven their angels continually see the face of my Father in heaven" (Matthew 18:10).

Activities
Tea Party

Have fun with the angel theme this day and have a Guardian Angel Tea Party. Make simple paper angels, hung from thread from light fixtures for decorations. Have children choose one small one to hang in their bedrooms.

Images of Angels

Display any angel statues or pictures on your Celebrations Table. Purchase fabric with angels on it (look in the Christmas section of a fabric store) for use as a cloth for this table.

Angel Snacks

Make an angel food cake for the party.
Prepare these cookies:

Angel Kisses

2 egg whites
1/2 cup sugar
1 teaspoon vanilla

Preheat the oven to 375 degrees. Whip the egg whites until frothy. Continue to beat while gradually adding the sugar and vanilla. When it forms stiff peaks, drop from a teaspoon onto a greased cookie sheet. Place them into the oven and immediately turn off the oven. Don't open the oven for at least 2 hours. Just before the party, have a child arrange the angel kisses on a plate.

Angel Napkins
If using paper napkins, have children draw angels onto the napkins before setting the table.

Story Book
At the tea party, read or look at the illustrations in *The High Rise Glorious Skittle Skat Roarious Sky Pie Angel Food Cake,* by Nancy Willard, while enjoying the cake. This is a enchanting story of a child who gets angelic help in making a birthday cake. The angels, while dignified, are something to see!

Story Time
Tell children stories from the book, *Where Angels Walk, True Stories of Heavenly Visitors,* by Joan Wester Anderson (Ballantine Books).

Guardian Angel Prayer
Learn the Guardian Angel prayer:
> Angel of God, my guardian dear,
> to whom God's love commits me here,
> ever this day, be at my side,
> to light and guard, to rule and guide. Amen.

October 4 – St. Francis of Assisi

One of the most beloved saints the world over is Francis of Assisi. Francis so loved God that he worked to have others come to love God, too. Francis rejoiced in life, and in the people and animals he met along the way. All this love and joy gives us many wonderful stories about him. Here is one of them.

There are two ways to use this story:

1) Make a copy of the illustrations for each child. The children can color them. Then cut out the pictures and mix them up. Next, read the text for the story aloud. As you read, have children place the pictures in the correct sequence.

2) Make a copy of both the illustrations and text for each child. Cut out. For each child, pile three 3" by 5" notecards, and fold in half to form a booklet. Staple the booklet on the fold of the middle pages. The pictures and texts can be matched up, sequenced, and glued onto the pages of the booklet.

ST. FRANCIS AND THE DOVES

St. Francis met a boy with doves in a cage. "Please let me have the doves," St. Francis said. The boy gave him the birds.

St. Francis began building nests for the doves.

The doves settled into the nests and laid eggs. Soon baby birds were peeping from the nest.

Every time St. Francis walked by the nests, doves would fly down and rest on his shoulders.

The birds would not leave him until St. Francis said a blessing for them. Then they flew off happily.

Harvest Story and Celebration Table

The harvest is here. Those who worked hard to plant and nurture gardens and fields through the summer are rewarded. As crops are gathered, we give thanks to a loving God who has blessed us with so much. The following story can help clarify this concept for young children, particularly those who have no experience with growing seasons.

As children enjoy guessing games, you can pause in your reading of the story before the fruit or vegetable in question is revealed, and offer children an opportunity to guess. If possible, provide the produce mentioned in the story and reveal each one as they are prayed for in the story. After the story, place these on the Celebration Table, to be touched and smelled. Provide tastes at another table.

Story: Aunt Rosie's Harvest

"I'm so glad you came," Aunt Rosie said, hugging Maggie, then Jake, and then Becca. "Your father always came for the harvest when he was your age. Now it's your turn. First, we have a prayer to thank God for all the good things we are harvesting this year. Then we have a feast to celebrate! Come on! To the garden!"

The children followed her, single file, to the large, sunny garden.

"What's 'harvest,' Aunt Rosie?" Jake asked.

"To harvest means to gather what's been growing in the garden. It's the time of year when most everything is ready to be picked and brought inside. Now, take hold of each other's hands, and close your eyes," Aunt Rosie instructed. She led them down the garden path.

"God has given us a vegetable that grows on a tall stalk. It's covered with green leaves on the outside that we pull off before we cook it. It has silky whiskers that we take off, too. We eat the inside, which is yellow—"

"Corn on the cob!" Maggie shouted, and they all opened their eyes.

"Yes!" Aunt Rosie said, snapping a plump cob off of a stalk. "Thank you, God the Creator, for the corn."

"Thank you, God!" said Maggie, Jake, and Becca.

"Now, hold hands and close your eyes again. Off we go!" Aunt Rosie said, and led the way to another part of the garden.

"God has given us a vegetable that grows underground. It is brown—or sometimes red or other colors—and rounded. We bake it, or boil it, or sometimes mash it—"

"Potatoes!" shouted Becca.

"Yes," said Aunt Rosie, plunging a pitchfork under a plant and pulling up several rounded, brown potatoes. "Thank you, God the Creator, for potatoes."

"Thank you, God," chorus Maggie, Jake and Becca.

"Now hold hands and close your eyes!"

They moved on. "God has given us a plant that yields a wonderful red fruit. We use it for spaghetti sauce, juice, ketchup—"

"Tomatoes!" Jake shouted.

"Yes," said Aunt Rosie, plucking a firm, warm tomato from the vine. "Thank you, God the Creator, for tomatoes."

"Thank you, God," said the children.

They moved on. Even with their eyes closed, they could feel they were near something very tall.

"God has given us a flower that started out as a tiny seed and soon grew to a plant taller than a person. Birds and people love the seeds—"

"Sunflowers!" shouted Jake.

"Yes," said his aunt, reaching up toward the huge flower head covered with circling rows of seeds.

Altogether they prayed, "Thank you, God, for the sunflowers."

Again they moved on. The children could smell many fragrances. "God has given us these plants, each with its own flavor, to add to our soups, and breads, to make tea—"

"Herbs?" asked Maggie.

"Yes," said Aunt Rosie. As she handed some basil to Maggie, rosemary to Jake, and thyme to Becca, they thanked God for the herbs.

Eyes closed, they moved to a place where some sprawling plants scratched their legs a little.

"God has given us a large plant, whose fruit is huge, round, and orange. We use it for pie, muffins and cookies—"

"Pumpkins!" squealed Becca. "My favorite thing in the whole garden!"

Aunt Rosie moved aside some prickly leaves. There sat a fat pumpkin, nearly orange, but streaked with a little green.

"Thank you, God, for pumpkins!" Becca shouted.

Aunt Rosie reached down and scooped up a handful of rich, brown soil. She held it out for the children to examine.

"Thank you, God the Creator, for soil, that takes the seeds we plant, feeds them and sprouts them, so we can have our potatoes, sunflowers, and pumpkins. And thank you for the rain and the sun, which nourishes our garden," Aunt Rosie prayed. "Now children, let's go back to the house for a harvest feast!"

"Will we have corn on the cob, Aunt Rosie?" Jake asked.

"That we will!"

"Thank you, God!" shouted Jake.

Celebration Table

October and harvest is an especially delightful time to use the Celebrations Table. Choose a cloth in harvest colors. Place fruits and vegetables on the table. Add sunflower seeds, acorns, colored leaves, etc. In browns and golds, make a sign that says, "Thank you, God the Creator, for the gifts from your earth." Hang this just above the table.

Sukkot, the Jewish Harvest Celebration

As our Christian roots lie deeply in Judaism, it is appropriate from time to time to teach children about a Jewish festival. Sukkot is a Jewish festival in autumn (September or October). It is a harvest celebration and a thanksgiving for the deliverance of the ancient Jews after their long years spent in the desert. To remember those desert years when the wandering people had to build makeshift huts for shelter at night, each year at this time some Jewish families build similar huts called sukkahs in their backyards, on flat rooftops or on porches. The roof is made of pine branches or strips of wood or fabric to encourage those inside to look up through the roof to the sky, stars and heavens above. Berries, garlands of flowers, grapes and corn adorn the walls to celebrate the year's abundance. Paper chains and pictures of Jerusalem can be added, too. Families and guests eat meals in their sukkahs and gather there to pray.

The table in the sukkah is laid with a bright cloth, and may hold a bowl of autumn fruits. Several more items can be added: a sheaf of palm frond, myrtle, and willow branches, bound together, forming a "lulav," and a citrus fruit called an etrog, a large, lemon-shaped food imported from Israel. Each day (except the Sabbath), these are waved in all directions, showing that God's goodness is all around. They are symbolic of the earth and harvest.

Activities
Scripture Story
Explain the festival of Sukkot to the children, perhaps reading to them the story of the Jews in the desert from a children's Bible.

Building a Sukkah
Bring in a refrigerator-size box for children to build a sukkah. Provide long strips of fabric or pine branches for the roof. Decorate with paper chains, gourds and pumpkins. Take turns having snack or lunch in your sukkah.

October 18 – St. Luke
One of the gospels as well as the Acts of the Apostles were written by Luke. He was a Greek man, well-educated, and was probably a doctor. He may also have been an artist. Luke never knew Jesus when he was on earth, but Luke became a student of Paul, who taught him all about Jesus. He also became Paul's friend and helper.

Most of the apostles and gospel writers were Jews who had begun to follow Jesus. Luke, however, was not Jewish. He understood best the people who were not Jews but still came to love Jesus. He wrote about this in his gospel. Many of the people he wrote about were poor and Luke's gospel is sometimes called, "The Gospel of the Poor." Luke also wrote often about Jesus and prayer. And, Luke shows us that Jesus' followers were often joyful and happy to give their lives doing Jesus' work.

Discussion Starter: Whom did Luke most often write about?

October

October 28 – Sts. Simon and Jude

Jesus chose twelve men to be His special helpers: Peter and Andrew, who were brothers, James and John, who were also brothers, Philip, Bartholomew, Thomas, Matthew, another James, Judas, and Simon and Thaddeus, who is also called Jude.

Today is the feast of Simon and Jude. It is believed that they both went to work in Persia, teaching others about Jesus where they died for their faith.

Long ago, there was a custom on this day for getting ready for All Souls' Day. Those who have died were especially remembered in early November. One way was to make a food called "soul cakes" to eat in remembrance. On the feast of Simon and Jude, people would go from door to door, begging for the ingredients for soul cakes. Standing in a doorway, the "beggars" would sing, "For the love of Simon and Jude, give us fixings for our food!"

Discussion Starter: What did people do on this feast to get ready for All Souls' Day?

October 31 – All Hallows' Eve

Halloween, a Christian term meaning "holy evening," has its roots in the British Isles of ancient times. The Celts divided the year into two parts, summer and winter. October 31 was celebrated as the last day of summer. It was called "Samhain," meaning "summer's end." It was believed that on this night of seasonal changes, the curtain between the living and the dead was particularly thin. Spirits could rise up and roam the earth on this night. For protection, the Celts carved faces into turnips and other root vegetables and placed candles inside, hoping this eerie lantern would frighten off any bad spirits. Some people also wore costumes or masks to fool the spirits into thinking they too were spirits to be avoided. When the Romans arrived, their customs of a harvest festival were added, with an emphasis on apples.

As with many other pre-Christian customs, Samhain became a Christian holiday. In 835, Pope Gregory IV sought to replace Samhain with All Saints' Day, followed by All Souls' Day.

Activities
The Cycle of Life

On All Hallows Eve, talk about the seasonal changes. Remind children that this seasonal dying leads to new life. Make charts of temperature changes; watch weather, note color changes in the leaves and sky. Read about birds migrating, and animals that hibernate.

Decorate Muffins

Serve children muffins thinly topped with orange frosting. Provide them with raisins, cereal, and candy corn to brightly decorate them.

November

November at a Glance

Dedication for November: The Souls in Purgatory
November's Liturgical Colors
Patron Saints of the Month
November 1: All Saints' Day
November 2: All Souls' Day
November 2: Feast, The Day of the Dead and Celebration Table Ideas
November 3: St. Martin de Porres
November 11: St. Martin of Tours
November 11: Veterans Day
November 16: St. Margaret Of Scotland
November 17: St. Elizabeth of Hungary
November 21: Feast of the Presentation of Mary
November 29: Anniversary of the Death of Dorothy Day
November 30: St. Andrew
Fourth Thursday: Thanksgiving

Dedication for November: The Souls in Purgatory

To "purge" means to cleanse or purify. Purgatory is the suffering of faithful people after death to rid them of all sin. With this, they achieve the holiness necessary to enter heaven. The *Catechism of the Catholic Church*, in #1054, refers to purgatory not as a place, but as a process. Pope Paul IV tells us that there is a link with those in heaven, those in the process of attaining heaven, and those still on earth. Amongst them is an exchange of all good things.

November's Liturgical Color

Ordinary Time: Green

Green is the color of hope and life.

Advent: Purple

Violet (or rose on the third Sunday)
The Advent colors symbolize waiting, penance and preparation.
The rose symbolizes subdued joy and repentance.

November

Patron Saints of the Month
November 3: Martin de Porres: hairdressers, those experiencing racial discrimination
November 11: Martin of Tours: beggars, soldiers
November 13: Francis Cabrini: migrants, hospital administrators, orphans
November 15: Albert the Great: medical technicians, scientists
November 16: Margaret of Scotland: Scotland, parents of large families, widows
November 17: Elizabeth of Hungary: bakers, homeless, medical workers, young brides
November 30: Andrew the Apostle: fishermen, Greece, Scotland

November 1 – All Saints' Day
"You shall love the Lord your God with all your heart, with all your soul, with all your strength and with all your mind and your neighbor as yourself" (Luke 10:27).

All Saints' Day is a holy day of obligation that honors all martyrs and saints known and unknown. A saint is a very blessed and holy person who loved God very much. Saints are people who dedicated their lives to God and served others unselfishly.

We believe that the first official observance of saints began with Pope Gregory III when he dedicated a chapel in the Basilica of St. Peter to "All the Saints." In 835 Pope Gregory IV ordered the Feast of All Saints be universally observed November 1.

Prayer
On this day dedicated to the saints of our church, we are thankful for their many good works and faithful love for God. How lucky we are to have such good people to learn from and look up to. Today as we honor the saints, we pray for guidance and courage and faith to also follow God in all we do each and every day. Amen.

Activities
Discussing Saints
Spend some time talking about the good works of saints and their faithfulness to God. Share some examples of people who are saints and the ways that they served other people and God. (Look ahead in this book to find many examples of sainted people.) Ask how we can act and live as the saints. How can we help others to do so? How can we take more time for prayer?

A Saint-a-Day
In the days or weeks before All Saints introduce your class to a different saint a day. Tell the story of the saint and talk about how that person shared and committed his/her life to God. Use the stories of the saints found throughout this book.

Pumpkin Art
As children of God we are all special individuals called to reflect God's love. Look up the meanings of the names of the children and

share them as a class. Write each child's name and its meaning on a pumpkin cut out from orange construction paper. Tie a piece of raffia around the top of the pumpkin and display in the room.

Ask your community for donations of real pumpkins late in October. Write each child's name and its meaning on individual pumpkins and send them home. Have each child in the class write their own name with permanent marker on a large pumpkin and display it in your prayer corner.

Future Saints

Have the children take turns tracing each other as they lay down on a large sheet of rolled paper. Each child cuts out their own outline and adds their names, facial features, hair etc. With adult help have the children draw or write positive attributes about themselves on the cutouts. Magazine pictures can also be used. Hang the completed life-size prints on a large wall in the hallway or your classroom. Label the display, "Future Saints" or "On Our Way to Sainthood."

November 2 – All Souls' Day

"For everything there is a season, and a time for every matter under heaven:

a time to be born, a time to die;

a time to plant, and a time to pluck up what is planted;

a time to kill, and a time to heal;

a time to break down, and a time to build up;

a time to weep, and a time to laugh;

a time to mourn, and a time to dance;

a time to cast away stones, and a time to gather stones together;

a time to embrace, and a time to refrain from embracing;

a time to seek, and a time to lose;

a time to keep, and a time to cast away;

a time to rend, and a time to sew;

a time to keep silence, and a time to speak;

a time to love, and a time to hate;

a time for war, and a time for peace."

Ecclesiastes 3:1-8

All Souls' Day follows All Saints' Day on November 2. It is a day dedicated to all who have died. Christians all over the world remember loved ones, family and friends with thanksgiving and prayer.

Prayer

Dear Lord,

Today we remember our loved ones, family and friends who have died and joined you in heaven. We are grateful for the joy and love these special people brought to our lives. With faith and hope we pray that our loved ones are at peace and enjoying eternal happiness in your loving care. Amen.

Activities
Discussion

Remind the children of any discussions you may have had regarding All Saints' Day. Let the children know that on All Souls' Day we remember all those who have died. We especially remember family members and friends. Depending on the age of your students you might want to spend a bit of time talking about what death is. Talk about the circle of life and the new life we have with Jesus when we die.

Book of the Dead

Many churches place a book of the dead in a very special place in their sanctuary. It is a place for community members to write the names of their loved ones who have died. The book is often displayed during the months of October and November. If your church has a book of the dead take the children to it and write the names of those close to them that have died in the book. Maybe you'd like to start a small book in your classroom for your prayer table. Don't forget that many children may have only experienced death involving a pet. Be sure to add the names of pets with other loved ones.

Centerpiece

Make a small candle centerpiece for the children to take home. Collect pint size canning jars for each child in the class. Put about an inch of sand or small pebbles in the bottom of the jar. Place a votive candle in the bottom of the jar. Place the cover on the jar and tie it with a piece of ribbon. Attach the above prayer to the jar and suggest that parents light the candle and pray together on All Souls' Day. Remind the children that the candle is only to be used with the help of parents.

New Life from Seeds

Take a walk to a church or community garden. Fall is the perfect time to look at the flowers that have died. Remind the children that in order for the flowers to make seeds to grow new flowers they must die. Out of the dead flower come the seeds that bring new life. If possible collect some of these seeds and save them to plant in the spring.

Grave Etchings

Encourage parents and children to go with grandparents or other family members to the cemetery to visit the gravestones of loved ones. This is a great opportunity to talk about death and the new life we all have in Jesus. Take a tracing of the name or names on the headstones.

November 2 – Feast, The Day of the Dead and Celebration Table Ideas

In the month of November, as harvests end and frost brings death to the natural world, the Catholic Church recognizes the importance of our own beloved dead, those who have "gone before" us. Different cultures bring especially intriguing celebrations to this remembrance.

Mexico

El Dia de los Muertos, or the "Day of the Dead," is a rich tradition for fondly remembering departed family members. It is a time to really feel their presence once again. The tradition involves both solemn and fun aspects. Traditional foods are eaten, altars are decorated in homes with pictures of those family members, and children receive candy, including sugar skulls. Families gather in the cemetery on November 2 to sing, talk, tidy graves, picnic and play games. As night falls, candles are lit, and families remain in the graveyard until dawn.

Philippines

Nine days before November 2, novenas are said for the holy souls. Every night in nearby cemeteries, people light candles, pray and decorate their family graves. Flowers are planted, crosses repainted, weeding done. The night before All Souls' Day, people pretending to be holy souls on their way to heaven go from door to door, asking for cookies and candy.

Poland

There are many superstitions about the return of spirits at this time. One that used to be held in rural Poland was that on midnight of All Souls' Day, the souls of all the departed parishioners would gather at the local church, where they had worshipped in life. Then, it was believed, the spirits visited scenes from their earthly life, especially their homes. Unafraid, the rural folk would leave doors and windows ajar in welcome.

Celebration Table

The Day of the Dead celebrations are wonderful customs for children who are just beginning to understand death. It is comforting for them to openly remember someone whom they loved. It is also helpful in giving children a sense of family history, for as adults fondly remember ancestors, children gain an appreciation of those whom they didn't know but who nonetheless have influenced their lives.

One way to create your own Day of the Dead tradition is by using the Celebration Table. This can be done both in the home and in the classroom. The autumnal colors and decorations, such as gourds or wheat can remain. Set on it a picture of one of your deceased family members. Have children bring in photos to the classroom. If you are doing this at home, help children set up additional family members' photos. Gather around this table and ask each person to tell something special they remember about the person in their picture. Encourage an atmosphere for fond memories. End with a short prayer of thanksgiving for these good people. Keep the pictures up at least for the first days of November or throughout the month.

November 3 – St. Martin de Porres

November is the month of two saints named Martin. Martin de Porres was born in Lima, Peru in 1597. He was very poor and treated badly by others because of his race. Martin was a very humble young man, but despite his meek ways and lowly status, Martin helped hundreds of people. He fed the hungry, counseled people, planted orchards on unused land so hungry people had fruit, began a home for street children, and healed people.

Discussion Starter: What can we do to help others?

November 11 – St. Martin of Tours

Martin of Tours was a Roman soldier who chose to become a "soldier of Christ" instead. As a priest and bishop, he taught many people about Jesus, began monasteries, and cured people.

There is a wonderful legend of the turning point in Martin's young life when he realized he must follow Jesus. Here it is, written in booklet format.

Martinmas

In some European towns, St. Martin Day, or Martinmas, is celebrated with a gathering of families at the church. Together they make lanterns that are fitted with candles. In the early evening darkness of November, a candlelight parade of children go through the streets, singing traditional St. Martin songs. This celebration ends with a pancake feast at the church. This tradition could be carried out at home or in a church community.

Activities
Reading the Booklet
Read the text from the booklet to the children. Discuss if Martin were here today, what do they think he would do to help people? Do they know anyone like Martin?

Assemble the Booklets
Give each child a copy of the booklet. They can color the illustrations. If they are able, have them cut out and assemble the booklets, too.

Story Sequencing
This booklet can be used for teaching story sequencing. Block out the page numbers on the pages of the booklet, copy the illustrations, and cut them into individual squares. Give each child a full set of illustrations, but in mixed order. On sheets of stiff paper, have them glue the story squares on in the correct sequence.

Sharing With Others
In honor of St. Martin, find a way to have the children experience sharing with someone they do not know well. Have a food drive in the classroom to take to a food pantry, bring toys to a family shelter, or create artwork for a nursing home.

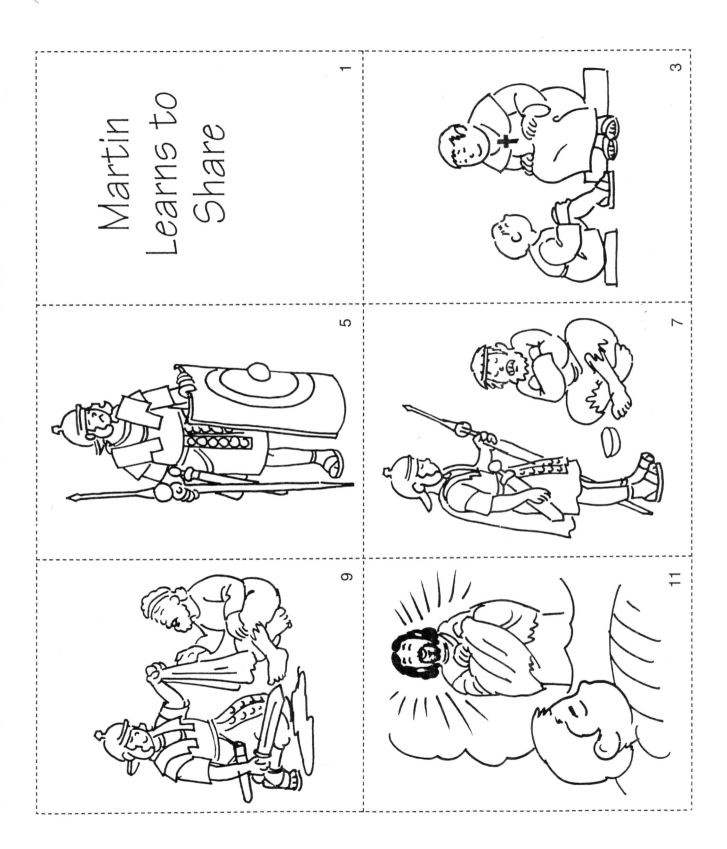

Martin
Learns to
Share

1

3

5

7

9

11

2

Long ago there lived a boy named Martin. His family did not believe in Jesus. Some Christians told Martin all about Jesus. He loved the stories of Jesus helping people who were poor and sick. Martin wanted to become a Christian. His parents said no.

4

When Martin was fifteen, his father had him become a soldier, but in his heart, he longed to be like Jesus.

6

One winter day when Martin was eighteen, he saw a man huddled by the city gates. The man was shivering, for he wore thin, ragged clothing. Maybe he was hungry and homeless too.

8

Martin thought of how Jesus helped people. Then Martin pulled off his warm soldier's cloak. With his sword, he cut the cloak in half. He put one half of the cloak over the shivering man's shoulders. He put the other half back on and went off to work.

10

That night, Martin dreamed he saw the poor man wearing the half cloak. When the man turned around, it was Jesus! Martin understood Jesus wanted him to become Christian and help others. And that is just what Martin did. Many people came to love Martin because of how he loved others.

November 11 – Veterans Day

"My fellow Americans, ask not what your country can do for you; ask what you can do for your country." (President John F. Kennedy)

Veterans Day is a day we honor men and women who have served and those who currently serve our country in the military. November 11 coincides with the end of World War I. On the 11th hour, of the 11th day, of the 11th month the Armistice (truce) was signed. World War I was called, "the war to end all wars." Veterans Day is a federal legal holiday.

Prayer

Dear Lord, today we take time to remember and give thanks for the many men and women who have served our country by working in the Army, Air Force, Navy, Marines and Coast Guard. We know that their jobs are not easy and require many sacrifices. Bless and keep the men and women and their families who have unselfishly served our country by committing themselves to the military. Amen.

Activities
Recognizing Military Persons

Talk a bit about the military and the role it has in keeping our country safe. Ask the children if they know of family members or friends who have served in the military.

Be sure the flag of the U.S. is hung outside your building today.

Extend an Invitation

Invite a veteran or current member of the military in to talk about their experiences.

Star Decorations

Cut out several red, white and blue, (six-inch) stars. Decorate the stars with a few foil star stickers. Send three or four stars home with each child. Include a note to parents asking them to write the names of family members on the stars who have served in the military. As the children return the stars, tape them to a red or blue ribbon and hang it across your prayer corner. During prayer on Veterans Day read the names on the stars and thank God for their service to our country.

November 16 – St. Margaret of Scotland

Margaret was the daughter of royal parents. A storm at sea cast her ship upon Scotland, which was a wild, rough, but beautiful place. The king, Malcolm, fell in love with and married the attractive, intelligent and deeply religious Margaret. As queen, she brought Christianity first to Malcolm, their children, and then to Scotland, along with education, trade and the arts. Margaret's generosity, wisdom, and work to bring God to all made her a beloved queen, mother and saint. Here is a story based on a legend about her.

Story: The Queen Loses Her Prayer Book

King Malcolm couldn't believe his luck. The smart, wise, and beautiful Margaret had agreed to become his wife and Scotland's queen! He loved her so much! But there was something he didn't understand. Each day she disappeared for an hour. She was warm and talkative the rest of the time, but the young king still wondered where she went.

"I'll follow her," he decided and set off.

She walked through the great woods and went into a cave. He crept closer. There he found Margaret had set up a little chapel for herself and she was praying! Quietly and respectfully, Malcolm entered and sat down with her. Margaret smiled. She opened her prayer book and began reading to him, teaching him the prayers. From then on, Malcolm prayed with Margaret and their love grew even stronger.

One day, before she left for the cave, she went for her prayer book as usual. It was not there. She looked and looked. What could have happened to it?

A bit sadly, she went to her cave without it. Malcolm met her there. He had a big grin on his face, and his hands were behind his back. "Missing something?" he asked.

From behind his back, he brought out Margaret's prayer book, but was it really her book? The covers, back and front, were now covered in jewels!

Margaret gasped, then reached for it, touching it gently. She looked up at Malcolm's smiling face. She understood that this gift was Malcolm's way of saying he loved her and he was beginning to understand her love of God.

Discussion Starter: What was Margaret doing every day when she disappeared for an hour?

November 17 – St. Elizabeth of Hungary

Today is the feast day of Elizabeth of Hungary. There is a famous legend about her that speaks of generosity, a good story that ties in well with Thanksgiving.

Story: Bread and Roses

Princess Elizabeth hurried down the hill, her cloak wrapped around her to hide the loaves of bread she carried. At the top of the hill was the castle of her husband Louis' family. Louis loved her, but she wasn't so sure about his family.

They were very rich, but all around them were poor people who did not have enough to eat. Elizabeth often took food from the family kitchen to feed others who were hungry. This angered the family, but Louis encouraged Elizabeth. "You are a good woman, Elizabeth, for all you do for others. No wonder I love you so much!" he frequently told her.

Someone was coming up the hill towards her. Elizabeth tensed up, afraid she would be caught with the bread. Then she saw that it was Louis.

"What are you hiding?" he teased her.

For a moment, Elizabeth felt confused. Was Louis beginning to agree with the rest of his family?

"Come on, show me!" he said, tugging at her cloak.

It opened, but no loaves of bread fell out. Instead, beautiful roses came tumbling down!

Elizabeth and Louis stared at the unexpected flowers at their feet.

"I did have bread—not roses!" Elizabeth whispered.

"This is a sign from God," Louis said. "You are a very holy woman, Elizabeth, and God must love you very much!"

Discussion Starter: What did Princess Elizabeth do for the poor? What did the bread turn into?

November 21 – Feast of the Presentation of Mary

Many of the celebrations of Mary are from the Eastern Church and this one began in Jerusalem in 543. It commemorates the ancient legend that when Mary was three years old, her parents brought her to, or "presented" her at the Temple to consecrate her to God's service. The point of this story is that Mary, from the very beginning of her life, was dedicated to God. Coming in late November, this feast also turns our thoughts to Advent, when we recognize that Mary herself is a Temple, where God came to dwell.

To recognize this feast, give children a length of shelf paper so they can draw the events of the following story. Draw vertical lines to divide the paper into four equal sections with the following themes.

Going to the Temple

1) An angel promised Anne and Joachim they would have a daughter. Mary was born to them. They were so happy!
2) When Mary was three years old, her parents took her to the Temple. There they would "present" her to God. The Temple was built on a hill. There were fifteen steps to climb to go inside.
3) Joachim put his little daughter down at the bottom of the steps. Happily she climbed up the steps all by herself. The High Priest kissed her and said, "Mary, God loves you and you shall do great things for all people. Forever after, people will know and love you!"
4) Little Mary danced with joy!

November 29 – Anniversary of the Death of Dorothy Day

When she was a child, Dorothy Day did not learn about religion. Her parents never took her to church. By the time she was 16, she said she didn't believe there was a God. However, by the time she died at age 83, Dorothy was considered by some to be one of the most interesting and powerful Catholics in the American Catholic Church.

The changes in Dorothy's life over the years helped her to come to believe in and love God, and to follow Jesus' teachings. Dorothy helped poor people, lived with them and lived like them. She worked hard for peace. She prayed. She is one of our best examples of someone who lived as Jesus had lived.

Discussion Starter: What did Dorothy Day do?

November 30 – St. Andrew

If you read the first chapter of the Gospel of Mark, you will meet St. Andrew. He was a fisherman and he worked with his brother, Simon (later Peter). It was when they were fishing that Jesus first saw them and called them to follow Him. At the miracle of the loaves and fishes, it was Andrew who found the boy who had the 5 loaves and 2 fishes.

Discussion Starter: What did Andrew do for a living?

The Fourth Thursday of November – Thanksgiving

"Oh, give thanks to the Lord for he is good; for his steadfast love endures for ever!" (Psalm 107:1)

Thanksgiving Day is a national holiday in the United States. It is a day set aside to give thanks to God for the many blessings of the year.

The first Thanksgiving was celebrated in 1619 by the Pilgrims who settled near the James River in Virginia. This was a Thanksgiving of prayer and did not include feasting, probably because there was so little to eat.

In 1721 after a successful harvest, Governor William Bradford planned a Thanksgiving celebration. The feasting lasted three days and included wild game, corn and other crops grown by the settlers. About ninety Native Americans also attended the celebration.

President Lincoln declared Thanksgiving Day to be observed on the fourth Thursday of November in 1863. It wasn't until 1941 that congress declared Thanksgiving Day to be a legal federal holiday.

Prayer

On this Thanksgiving Day, we thank God for all of the blessings in our lives. We are thankful for the people who love us and take care us as we learn and grow. We are thankful for friends with whom we share secrets and play and laugh. We are thankful for the food we eat, the warm clothes we wear and the loving home in which we live. Thank you, Lord, for all of these blessings. In Jesus' name we pray. Amen.

Activities
Sharing Traditions
Discuss the Thanksgiving holiday with the children. Have them share a tradition their family

has for this holiday. At prayer time invite the children to individually add some specific things they are thankful for.

Paper Thanksgiving Chains

Make a list of things with the children that they are thankful for. Write these on strips of orange and yellow paper and link them together to make a paper chain. Hang the chain around the room.

Mini-Pumpkins

Purchase mini pumpkins from the grocery store; they are about fifty cents each. Tie a piece of raffia around the stem of the pumpkin and attach a card with a copy of the Thanksgiving prayer.

Pumpkin Candleholder

Make a mini pumpkin candleholder. Use a carving knife to cut out a 1" hole in the center of the pumpkin. Place a taper or votive candle in the pumpkin. Use either of these ideas to decorate your classroom or send them home for the kitchen table.

Food for the Poor

Collect food for the local food pantry. To make the collection more interesting, collect only baby food or breakfast food. Assign each family a couple of nonperishable items for a thanksgiving dinner. Suggestions would be canned gravy, vegetables, cranberries, stuffing, pie, cake or bread mixes, juices and relishes.

Decorating Bags and Boxes

Decorate warehouse grocery boxes or other cardboard boxes with thanksgiving greetings or a prayer. Add drawings made by the children to make them look festive. Give these to your local food pantry to use for distributing food. Decorating grocery bags is also fun.

Hoop Art

Have the children look through magazines and cut out pictures of the things they are thankful for. Tape the pictures around a Hula-Hoop and hang it in the room. The hoop could hang on its side like a wall wreath or from the ceiling, parallel to the ground. To hang the hoop from the ceiling, tie three, 4-foot pieces of string onto the hoop, making sure they are equal distance apart. When tying leave one end of the string as long as possible. Gather the long ends of the string together and tie in place. Hang the hoop in your prayer corner just above the eye level of the children.

Story: A Story of Thankfulness

Today Gyles was wonderfully happy. Ever since he had come by ship to this new land, he had been hungry and cold. There was never enough food for all his people. But with the help of their new friend, Squanto, Gyles' people had been able to raise enough food for this winter. Now they were celebrating to give thanks to God.

Some of the grown-ups had been cooking for days, and now, Gyles noticed, their new friends, the Wampanoag (WAHM-peh-NOH-ag) people, had arrived for the celebration. They brought food to contribute to the feast.

And what a feast it was! Gyles saw plates of steaming hot venison, or deer meat. There was delicious wild turkey, and large, juicy geese, all ready to be sliced. From the ocean had come clams, eels and fish called bass.

Gyles had been working all morning, fetching water and gathering firewood. Now he sat down at a long table with some of the Wampanoag guests who could speak his language. He could not speak theirs. He liked them, and wanted to stay as close as he could.

There was even more food: water cress and leeks, dried gooseberries, strawberries, cherries and plums! Soon his plate was heaping with food, and he barely had room for the cornbread.

They ate for a long time. Then they played games and danced. Nothing could be better than this, Gyles thought.

Then something even more wondrous happened. One of his new friends motioned for Gyles to come closer to the fire. He poured some corn kernels into an earthen jug and smiled at Gyles. He seemed to be waiting for something, so Gyles waited too.

Pop! Pop! Gyles was startled. The corn had burst into little white puffs! The popping continued until all the corn was white and puffy. Gyles had never seen popcorn before. Then his friend carefully poured maple syrup over the popped corn, and made a small ball. He handed it to Gyles. Gyles touched it with his tongue. Ah, it was sweet! He took a bite. How crunchy it was! It was delicious. His friend smiled again, enjoying Gyles' happiness. Gyles took another bite. He looked around at his new home and new friends. He heard all the laughter of the others. He tasted this new treat. And he was very thankful for all of God's blessings.

Activities
Thanksgiving Puzzles

Enlarge the puzzle on page 62 and make copies for each child. Back the copied puzzles onto tagboard before cutting into pieces. After you have read the story once, hold up the pieces of your puzzle, naming the pictures on each one. Then, with children at tables with their own puzzles, tell the story again, encouraging them to find the pieces that correspond to the story. The very youngest may not be able to put the puzzle together, but they can enjoy identifying the pieces.

Thanksgiving Story Booklet

The puzzle could also be used to make a Thanksgiving story booklet. Cut out the puzzle pieces, eliminating the puzzle lines so just the drawings remain. Give each child a booklet made of 14 pieces of paper. On page 1, the cover, print "A Thanksgiving Surprise." On page 2, have children glue the drawing of the venison and add the words, "When the Pilgrim and Wampanoag peoples had their feast they had venison." On page 3, glue the picture of the turkey, and add the words "wild turkey." Page 4, "the geese," and so on. On the last page, glue the larger picture of the popcorn and the words "and there was a surprise for the children: popcorn balls!"

Thanksgiving Snacks
This story offers these snack possibilities:
Serve popcorn or popcorn balls.
Let children taste real maple syrup.
Make a simple cornbread and serve with syrup.

Celebration Table
You can add a thanksgiving theme to the Table, which is already set as a Remembering Table. To the pictures of deceased loved ones, for which you are thankful, you can add food items and other things that symbolize what you are thankful for.

Project Checklist

_____
_____
_____
_____
_____
_____
_____
_____
_____
_____
_____
_____
_____
_____

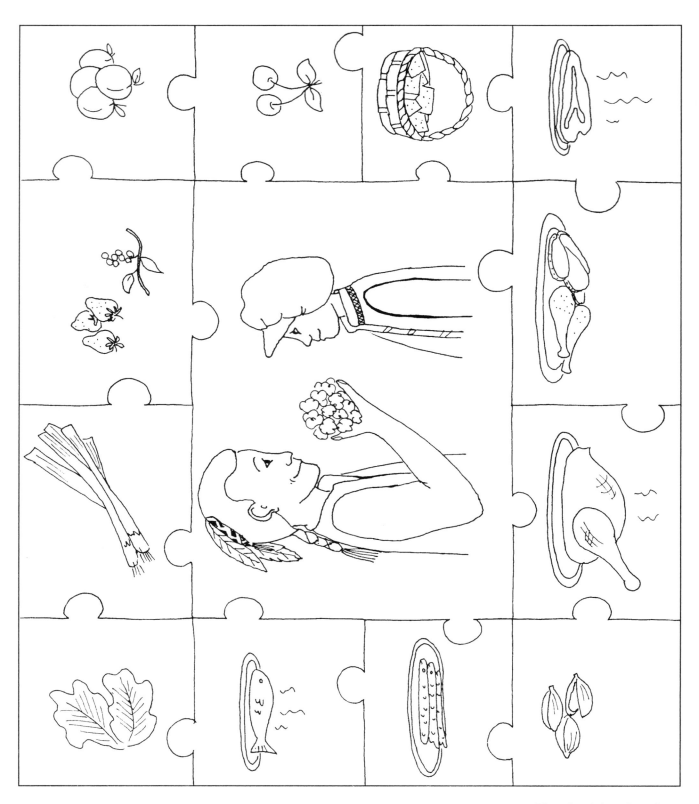

Thanksgiving Puzzle

December / Advent / Christmas

December / Advent / Christmas at a Glance

Dedication for December: The Immaculate Conception
Liturgical Colors
Patron Saints of the Month
Celebrations Table for December/Advent
Season of Advent
December 6: Feast of St. Nicholas
December 8: Feast of the Immaculate Conception
December 13: St. Lucia Day
December 21: 1st Day of Winter
Saint Francis and the First Crèche
The Christmas Candle Tradition
December 24: Christmas Eve
December 25: Christmas Day
Christmas Booklet
Christmas Peace
A Christmas Legend
December 26: Feast of St. Stephen
December 27: Feast of St. John the Evangelist and Apostle
December 28: Feast of the Holy Innocents
1st Sunday after Christmas: Feast of the Holy Family

Dedication for December: The Immaculate Conception

Mary, Jesus' mother, is such a special person; she was chosen by God to be without any sin all her life.

December/Advent/Christmas Liturgical Colors

Advent: Purple

The Advent colors symbolize waiting, penance and preparation.

Christmas: White

The Christmas color symbolizes joy.

December

Patron Saints of the Month
December 3: Francis Xavier: patron of missions, Borneo
December 4: Barbara: architects, builders, the dying, miners, prisoners
December 6: Nicholas of Myra: children, brides, Greece, merchants, sailors
December 7: Ambrose: learning
December 8: The Immaculate Conception: Brazil, Portugal, United States
December 12: Our Lady of Guadalupe: North America and South America
December 13: Lucy: eye diseases
December 26: Stephen: bricklayers, deacons
December 27: John: Asia Minor (Turkey)
December 28: The Holy Innocents: babies

Celebrations Table for December/Advent
The table can reflect this holy time in several ways. Use a dark blue-violet cloth, or a dark blue cloth that is strewn with stars to symbolize the darkest time of the year and the years of darkness while the Jewish people waited for the Messiah. The table can be used to focus on the saints of Christmas time, particularly St. Nicholas and St. Lucia. Place a statue or holy card of Nicholas on the table and ask children to bring in cans of food to be donated to a food pantry, telling them of Nicholas' generosity as well as his concern for those who do not have what they need. The food can be on the table for a few days.

St. Lucia is associated with light. On her feast day, place a statue or picture and one candle. Add another candle each day until Christmas. Explain that Jesus is the Light of the World, and saints help us know his Light.

The table can also be used as the setting for an Advent wreath. It is a simple but powerful symbolism of the four week wait until Christ's birthday.

Another use for the table would be the placement of a child-proof Christmas crèche. In the beginning of Advent, place only the empty stable. As the days go by, add sheep, shepherds, other animals, the magi coming from the east, and Mary and Joseph traveling across the table towards the stable. Add the manger and Baby Jesus last.

Season of Advent
"Prepare the way of the Lord, make straight his paths." Matthew 3:3

The beginning of the church year is marked with the season of Advent. The word "Advent" comes from the Latin word "Adventus" with means arrival or coming. Traditionally Advent begins on the Sunday nearest St. Andrew's feast day, which is November 30, and observed on the four Sundays before Christmas on December 25. The Advent season is one of anticipation, reflection and hope as we wait for the arrival of Jesus.

Prayer
Be with us, Lord, as we enter this waiting season of Advent. We thank you for the many blessings in our lives and with anticipation, preparation and hope we look forward to the arrival of the your Son, Jesus, the light of the world. Amen.

Activities
The Advent Wreath

The use of the Advent wreath with four candles has been an Advent ritual for hundreds of years. The Advent wreath is a symbol of the 4-week wait for Jesus' birth. The green branches remind us of the new life we have in Jesus, the circle represents the eternity of God's love for us (with no beginning and no end), and the candles represent the light and hope Jesus brings into a dark world.

Set up an Advent wreath in your classroom and use the prayers to observe the season with the children you teach. Or, pray with a living Advent wreath explained below.

A Living Wreath

Make a living Advent wreath with your children as you observe Advent. Use a 12' length of green garland. Cover 4 wrapping paper tubes or potato chip cans with purple paper and cut out 4 large flames from yellow paper. For each week in Advent add a flame to another candle. As you pray the Advent prayers have the children stand in a circle holding the green garland. Give four of the children a candle to hold. As you begin your prayer tape the flame to the candle. Add a flame to each candle as the weeks go by during Advent.

• Prayer for Week 1

As we light the 1st candle on our Advent wreath we start down a holy path to Christmas. We give thanks to God for all of the good things in our lives, especially the love of our family and friends. We are happy to share God's love with others while we are preparing to celebrate the birth of Jesus, God's Son. We ask that you help us stay on the Advent path and keep our hearts focused on Jesus as we prepare for Christmas. Amen.

• Prayer for Week 2

Mary and Joseph were people of great love. They were chosen to be the parents of Jesus because of their love for God. We are thankful to have their obedience, kindness and deep faith as our examples. As we travel on our Advent path and light the 2nd candle on the Advent wreath, we pray that we too will love God as much as Mary and Joseph. Amen.

• Prayer for Week 3

The journey to Bethlehem must have been very hard for Mary and Joseph. A long donkey ride on a rough path must have seemed to go on forever, but Mary and Joseph trusted God and knew that God would be there to take care of them. We are so thankful that God is always here for us, during good times and bad. We remember this when we light the 3rd candle on our Advent wreath. As we continue on the Advent path we ask God to be with us in all we do each day. Amen.

December

• *Prayer for Week 4*

How excited Mary and Joseph must have been as the day of Jesus' birth grew closer! Their hearts must have been full of joy and thanksgiving. As we light the 4th candle on our Advent wreath and Christmas Day comes closer, we too have become more excited and joyful. Be with us loving God and help us continue to keep Jesus in our hearts as our Advent path takes us closer to Christmas. Amen.

Gift Tags

Make gift tags as a service project during Advent. Collect used Christmas cards from parents and others in your community. Ask a volunteer to cut off the backs of the cards and sort through them so that the backside of all of the pictures is blank. Set up a workstation and have the children punch holes in an upper corner of each card. Have older children tie a ribbon through each hole. Put six tags in a zip lock bag and give them to members of the community. Sell the tags and donate your earnings to a "Toys for Tots" program.

Toy Workshop

Set up a toy workshop in your classroom. Ask the children to bring in next-to-new toys that they have outgrown. Set up a center with wet wipes, tape, toothbrushes, etc. and have the children fix and clean up the toys. Donate the toys to a school or center in your community for their use or check with a homeless shelter for needs they may have.

Scavenger Hunt

Plan a magazine scavenger hunt. Have the children search through old November and December magazines to find pictures of Advent and Christmas symbols. Choose four to six symbols and place a picture of each on a large piece of construction paper attached to a shoebox. As the children find the symbols, they cut them out and place them in the correct box. Use these pictures to make holiday cards or place mats. Suggestions for symbols include candles, trees, lights, nativity scenes, stars, angels or gifts.

Nativity Scene

Put together a life-size nativity scene for a wall in a hallway or large meeting space. Assign each child a character out of the nativity story. If you have a large group, assign several shepherds and angels. Have the children take turns tracing each other's  body for their character from the story on large paper. After the body is cut out, allow a lot of time to dress the character to fit the role. Use paper scraps, crayon, wrapping paper, etc. for clothes. To make halos staple tree garland or wire stars shaped in a circle to the top of the heads.

Use yarn for hair and sequins to decorate crowns. The sky is the limit on how far you go. Use crepe paper to outline a stable and paper cut outs to make the manger bed for baby Jesus. To make Jesus, trace a toddler or a baby doll one of the children owns. Tape the figures inside and around the stable. Add stars to the sky as well as trees and hills. If you have extra time have the children make sheep and cows, etc. Be sure the children put their names on their figures so that they can take them home later in the season.

Recycled Ornaments

Make recycled tree ornaments for the children to take home. Spray the small pieces of puzzles that are not being used any more with gold, red or green spray paint. When dry have the children glue these to Christmas symbols cut out of box cardboard also painted with spray paint.

Add a bit of glitter paint to the ornaments and allow to dry. Punch a hole in the top of the ornament and lace a ribbon through for hanging.

December 6 – St. Nicholas

St. Nicholas was a well-loved bishop born in the fourth century in the country now known as Turkey. His family was very wealthy and both of his parents died when he was very young. St. Nicholas is remembered for his very generous spirit. He always helped others and gave most of his inheritance away. St. Nicholas once helped a father who could not afford to take care of his three oldest daughters. The father did not know what to do. Nicholas found out and left money in the daughters' shoes that were drying outside of the house. Thus the tradition of leaving shoes at the doorstep for St. Nicholas to fill on December 6.

Here is yet another story of how St. Nicholas helped others:

In the city by the sea, the people were hungry because so little food had grown that year. One day, a ship came into the harbor, filled with grain for the powerful emperor. Bishop Nicholas went to the ship's captain. "My people need food, and the emperor has plenty," Nicholas said. "Please give us some grain. I promise you will not have any missing when you get to the emperor." This was impossible! And, the captain would be punished when the emperor found the grain missing. Still, he left some grain for the people. That grain supply lasted until food grew once again! And, the ship was not missing any grain! Bishop Nicholas miraculously kept his promise.

Prayer for St. Nicholas Day

Today we remember the generous spirit of St. Nicholas. He loved God and shared his devotion to God by helping people in need and putting others before himself. Dear God, we ask you to help us learn from the example of St. Nicholas. Help us to share kind words, our toys, and the games we play with those around us. We offer you this prayer with generous and loving hearts. Amen.

December

Activities

Filling Shoes With Candy

A favorite tradition on St. Nicholas Day is to have the children leave one shoe outside the classroom door. Have an adult friend leave a few candies, gold chocolate coins, a prayer card, pencil or small toy in each shoe.

Shoe Blessing

Celebrate with a shoe blessing before the children leave their shoes outside the door. Have the children sit in a circle and put one shoe in the center. Call the children a few at a time to retrieve a shoe (other than their own) from the pile of shoes in the circle. After everyone has a shoe they quietly look to see whose shoe they have. Start the blessing by having one person say,

"May God bless you today_____ (the child's name) with a kind and giving heart just like St. Nicholas."

as they return the shoe they have to its owner. The second child then returns the blessing to the first child. The second child then passes the shoe he or she has to its owner with the same blessing. The third child returns the blessing and on it goes until everyone has his or her own shoe back.

Holiday Service Project

Begin a holiday service project with a collection of socks on St. Nicholas Day. Encourage families to send in new socks in child and adult sizes for the children to fill. Before filling the socks, put one sock inside the other. This will keep the pairs of socks together. Fill the socks with soaps, toothbrushes, wrapped candy, small toys, pens, prayer cards, printed Band-Aids, etc. After filling them gather the top of the sock together and tie with a ribbon. Deliver to your local shelter.

Bishops' Hats

Make bishops' hats (Miters) for the children to wear in class on this special day. Use the pattern on page 69, tracing it on colored paper to make the front of the bishop's hat. Cut out a gold cross and glue to the front of the hat. Staple or tape this to a strip of construction paper about 2" wide and 24" long. Adjust to fit on each child's head.

Candy Canes

Share candy canes with the children and talk with them about the symbolism of the shape of the cane. Jesus was often called the Good Shepherd. A shepherd uses a cane or long hook to guide the sheep back to the fold or rescue. As a bishop, St. Nicholas carried a staff as a symbol of his relationship with God and the people he served. Bishops today still carry the staff when celebrating with the community.

Follow-up by making candy canes by twisting a red and white pipe cleaner together. Send them home with a brief explanation.

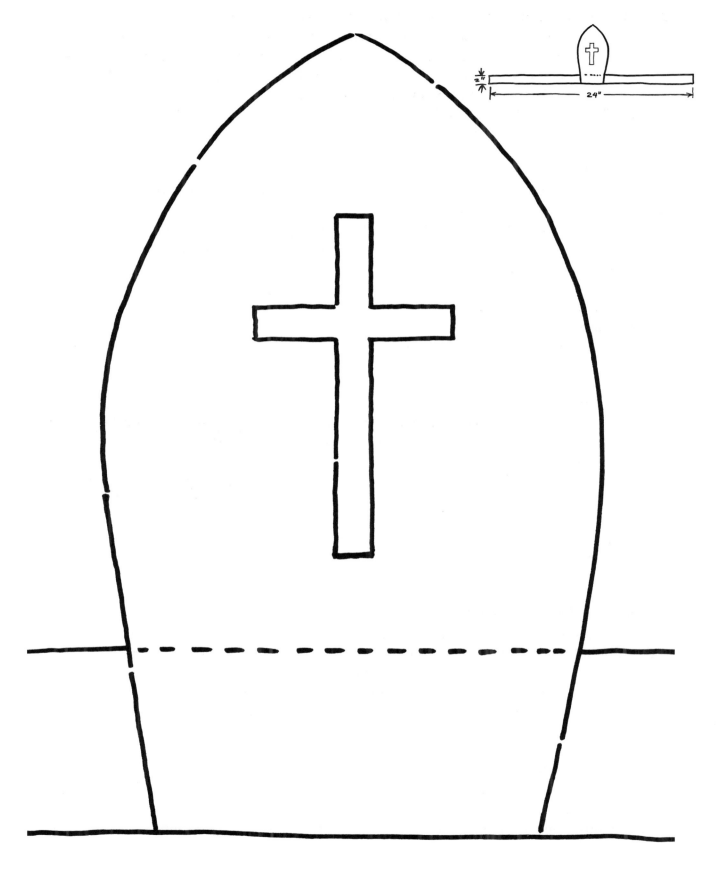

December 8 – Feast of the Immaculate Conception

On this day we celebrate and honor the holiness and innocence of Mary. As Catholics we believe that Mary was at her conception free of sin. She was free of original sin and therefore pure enough to be the mother of Jesus. The feast of the Immaculate Conception is a holy day of obligation and all Catholics are encouraged to attend Mass.

Pope Pius the IX defined the official teachings of the church regarding the Immaculate Conception of Mary on December 8, 1854.

Prayer to Mary

Holy Mary, Mother of Jesus, we honor you on this special day. You were born to grow up to be the mother of Jesus. What an awesome job! As we remember you today, we ask that you help us to love God with all of our hearts. You accepted God's plan for your life without hesitation and we ask that we too will be able to accept God's plan for our lives. In your Son, Jesus' name we pray, Amen.

Activities

Pilgrimage

If you have an area of your Church building dedicated to Mary, take the children there to pray.

Paper Chain

Honor Mary's purity by making a white paper chain with white cutout flowers to decorate the prayer space. Write each child's name on a flower or link of the chain.

Discussion

Talk about how life might have been for a young girl like Mary to grow up 2000 years ago. Compare it to our lives today.

December 13 – St. Lucy

St. Lucy (or, in Scandinavia, Lucia), whose name means light, was often called the patron saint of the light of the body or the eyes. People prayed to her for help with eye diseases. In Scandinavia, St. Lucia's feast day is celebrated by the oldest daughter in the family serving a special breakfast (including Lucia Cakes) wearing a white robe and a ring of candles around her head. On this day, young boys often wore Star Boy hats that were blue cones covered in gold stars.

Prayer for St. Lucia Day

As we gather today we light a candle to remember the love St. Lucia shared with others. She looked to the light of Jesus for strength, guidance and hope. As we prepare for Christmas, remind us to also look to Jesus, and be a reflection of His light to those around us. Amen.

Activities
Crown of Candles

Make a crown of candles for the girls to wear as you share the prayer above. Cut out a green strip of paper about 3" by 18" and staple in place to fit each girl's head. Have them cut out at least 4 candles and glue them around the green headband. Glue a copy of the prayer for St. Lucia to the front of the ring.

Star Hat

On St. Lucia's Day the boys wear a Star Hat. Roll a piece of 18" by 12" paper into a large cone. After stapling the hat into place, round off and trim the lower edge. Have the boys put silver and gold star stickers on the outside of the hat or cut stars out of white and gold paper to glue on the outside.

Eye Reminders

Wear sunglasses today to help the children remember that St. Lucia is the patron saint of the eyes.

Flashlight Tag

Play flashlight tag. Turn off the lights in the room and have everyone find a hiding place. Assign one spot in the center of the room to be the Lucia or safe place. One person is given a flashlight and he or she tries to shine it on the other children as they try to reach the safe place. The first person to reach the goal or safe place gets to use the flashlight for the next round.

Special Lucia Day Snack

Serve muffins or sweet bread and hot chocolate for snack using special dishes and a teapot as a reminder of the Swedish custom of serving a special breakfast on St. Lucia's Day.

December 21 – 1st Day of Winter

The 1st day of winter falls on the shortest day of the year, which is December 21. We have the least amount of sunlight on this day and after this day the days start to get longer again.

Prayer for the 1st Day of Winter

Dear Lord, we thank you for the change in seasons. What fun we have bundling up to play in the snow and cold (change this line to reflect your weather). On this shortest, darkest day of the year, we are reminded that in a few days we will soon be celebrating the birth of Jesus, the Light of the World. Amen.

Activities for Cold, Snow-Covered Climates
Winter-Fun Discussion

Talk about winter and the changes we see in the weather. Discuss what is most fun about winter and what isn't.

December

Winter-Time Blessing

Sprinkle a bit of silver or iridescent glitter in each child's cupped hands or shoes as you offer a blessing at the end of your winter prayer and discussion.

Paper Mittens

Have the children cut out a pair of paper mittens. Punch a hole at the top of each mitten and lace a piece of yarn through each hole. Have the children write something they are thankful for in winter, such as warm fires, snowmen, ice-skating, sliding, etc. on one of the mittens. To make the mittens more memorable, have the children make a handprint with tempera paint on the backside of each mitten. Be sure to add names and dates to the handprints.

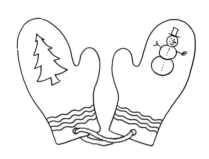

Snowflakes

Make large snowflakes out of white construction paper and decorate them with glitter or puffy paint. Hang these on the windows or from the ceiling in your classroom.

Snowpeople

Make snowpeople for each child in the class. On dark blue paper, have the children make a snowman or woman with cotton balls or cut outs of leftover lace. Use movable eyes, buttons or beads to finish the project.

Placemats

Glue smaller snowflakes or doilies to dark blue paper. Laminate the paper or cover it with clear contact and use as placemats throughout the winter.

Activities for Warm Climates
Indoor Snowpeople

If you live in a part of the country that doesn't get much snow, make indoor snow people to enjoy throughout the season. Fill large white trash bags (the kind without extra ties) with wrinkled up sheets of newspaper. Tie a twist tie at the top of the bag. To make smaller sizes put less newspaper in the bags. Staple or tape the "balls of snow" on a wall or bulletin board. Add hats, stick arms, mittens and facial features. Use the real items or paper cut outs.

Marshmallow Snowpeople

Make marshmallow snowpeople for a sweet winter snack. Make white frosting and drop a small spoon of it on a Graham Cracker

Square or flat cookie. Place a marshmallow on the frosting and add 1 or 2 more marshmallows with frosting in between to the first one. Dip small candies in frosting to make facial features, hats etc.

Bird Feeders

Make bird feeders for the birds that sometimes have a hard time finding food in the winter. Spread peanut butter on both sides of a bagel. Dip the bagel in birdseed until it is completely covered. Put a piece of yarn through the middle of the bagel and tie the two ends together to make a loop for hanging. During outside playtime have the children hang their bird feeders on trees or shrubs.

St. Francis and the First Crèche

In many parts of the world, simple or elaborate manger scenes, or crèches, are displayed in homes, churches, schools, and stores. We would not have this lovely custom if it were not for St. Francis of Assisi. Francis was concerned that many people did not truly understand Christ's birth: the poverty of the circumstances and the significance of God becoming human. With the help of his friend, Giovanni, Francis recreated the scene at the stable. There it seems, a miracle occurred for Francis. Read this story aloud after setting up your crèche together.

Story: St. Francis and the Baby in the Manger

It was Christmas Eve. The holy man named Francis and his friend Giovanni stood with the townspeople of Greccio in a cave in the nearby hills. All around them, torches and candles danced light and shadows on the people's faces. A few days before, Francis had asked Giovanni to set up the cave to look like the stable Jesus had been born in hundreds of years before. It even had a manger with hay so people could see what kind of bed little Jesus had slept in.

Francis planned to have Christmas Eve Mass in the stable that Giovanni had created. Francis sang and preached. His voice was filled with his love for Jesus. Giovanni listened with his heart as well as with his ears. He saw Francis go over to the hay-filled manger and gently touch the rough wooden box. Then Giovanni blinked. Could it be? Could there be a sleeping baby in the manger? It had been empty only seconds before, but Giovanni thought he saw a baby! Francis went on talking, but tenderly touched the baby, who stirred and woke. Giovanni stared. Francis had awakened the Christ Child!

The others around them sang more joyfully. Giovanni was not certain if they too saw the Child but he joined in with their songs. Then the manger was empty again, but everyone's hearts were full. The singing went on into the night. The service ended but never the joy.

And now, hundreds of years later, many people set up mangers and stables, just as Giovanni helped Francis do, so long ago.

Discussion Starter: Whom did Giovanni see in the manger?

The Christmas Candle Tradition

People in the Slavic nations, Poland, the Ukraine, and Russia, often make a large Christmas candle for a table centerpiece. It is customary to have it blessed at church. When a loaf of bread is used as its candleholder, it is a symbolic reminder of Christ, the Light of the World.

Activity: *Bread Dough Candleholder*

Make a Christmas candleholder by using sections of frozen bread dough. Give each child approximately a ten-inch square section of thawed bread dough. Help each child manipulate the dough so that one side is flat and other slightly rounded. Place each mold of bread dough on individual pieces of tin foil. Use a permanent marker to put each child's initials on the tin foil that is under his or her bread mold and place on cookie sheets. Bake the bread at 350 until golden brown. Cool and invite your priest to come in and bless the bread. Send the bread home with a family note, explaining the tradition and blessing, along with an 8-inch taper candle for the center of the family's table.

December 24 – Christmas Eve

And in that region there were shepherds out in the field, keeping watch over their flock by night. And an angel of the Lord appeared to them, and the glory of the Lord shone around them, and they were filled with fear. And the angel said to them. "Be not, afraid; for behold, I bring you good news of a great joy which will come to all the people; for to you is born this day in the city of David a Savior, who is Christ the Lord. And this will be a sign for you: you will find a babe wrapped in swaddling cloths and lying in a manger." Luke 2,8-12

The first December Christmas observance recorded was found on a Roman calendar around A.D. 336. Historians believe that the Christmas customs and celebrations that help us celebrate the coming of Jesus grew out of harvest celebrations held in December. Europeans celebrated the end of the harvest season with special foods, decorations, singing and gift giving and so began the first Christmas traditions.

Christmas Eve Prayer

On Christmas Eve we celebrate the birth of Jesus, God's Son, born in a humble stable. We think about His parents who must have been scared and tired, but also full of joy as they held their new baby boy in their arms for the first time. Thank you, Lord, for sending us your Son, Jesus, who gives us light and hope in the days ahead. We ask that you guide our family (families) to be a reflection of the holy family in all we say and do, each and every day. Amen.

Activities
Jesus in the Manger

Place baby Jesus in the manger of your nativity scene. Using the figures in the scene tell the story of Jesus' birth with your children. Talk about what it must have been like for Mary and Joseph to have their baby in a barn without clean sheets, lights, running water and heat. What do you think they said to each other after Jesus was born?

Family Traditions

Share family traditions. Talk with the children about who they spend the holiday with, where they go, what they eat and how they open presents, etc.

Christmas Story Reenactment

Dress everyone up in bathrobes and dish towels and act out the Christmas story. Take a family picture of your holy family to enjoy throughout the year.

Jesus Light

Send home a votive candle in a clay flowerpot. Add sand to the bottom of the pot and place the candle in the middle. Include instructions for families to place the pot on the front porch step or by the front door to light the way for baby Jesus. Add the above Christmas prayer.

Pickle in the Tree

Play the German pickle game. Hide a glass or paper pickle in the Christmas tree. The first person to find the pickle in all of the decorations wins a prize. That person then hides the pickle for the next round of the game.

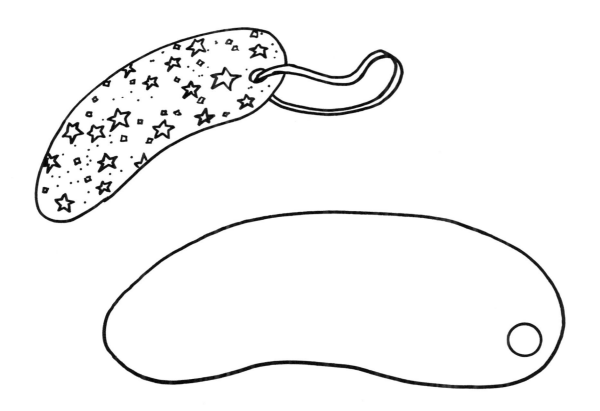

December 25 – Christmas Day

"Glory to God in the highest, and on earth peace among men with whom he is pleased!" Luke 2:14

What a wonderful gift God gave us on Christmas. For over 2000 years Christians have celebrated the birth of God's Son in a lowly stable in Bethlehem.

Christmas Prayer

Dear Lord, as we gather with family and friends on this happy day, we remember the gift of the baby Jesus born 2000 years ago in Bethlehem. We are thankful for our family and friends who have come together with love and joy to celebrate the gift of Jesus. Be with us today and help us keep the love and joy we feel in our hearts with us all year long. In Jesus' name we pray. Amen.

Activities
Pre-Meal Reading

Read the story of Jesus' birth from the Bible or picture book before snack or the family meal.

Special Christmas Gifts

A few days before Christmas ask the children to fill out gift cards for each member of their family thanking them for the gifts they bring to the family (humor, helpfulness, cooking, listening). Put the tags in a gift bag and encourage families to share them on Christmas Day.

Candy Pots

Use the following idea as a party favor or student gift. Purchase small two-inch, clay flower pots. Spray the outside of the pots with silver or gold paint. Fill the pot with foil wrapped candies and insert a candy cane in the center. Gather a piece of cellophane around the pot and tie it at the top with a piece of ribbon. Add a gift tag with a Christmas blessing on each.

Christmas Booklet
When Jesus Was Born

The time shortly before the Christmas celebrations begin can be very difficult for young children. Channel some of the excitement and energy by making a booklet that will help the children focus on the Nativity story. You can use any size paper, crayons, markers, pencils, etc. Tell the following Nativity story, pausing as the children illustrate each page. Staple the pages together. Or, use the patterns provided to help with the illustrating.

This booklet would make a good last-minute gift. Also, the story could be drawn instead onto shelf paper and displayed on a wall.

(Cover) WHEN JESUS WAS BORN
(Page 1) Long ago, the angel Gabriel visited a young woman called Mary. "God loves you, Mary!" Gabriel said. "You will have a baby boy. He will be God's Son. Name him Jesus."

Mary said, "I will do as God asks."

(Page 2) Mary told Joseph, the man she would soon marry, about the special baby. "I will help you take care of the baby," Joseph said. "But before he is born, we must go on a journey to the town of Bethlehem."

(Page 3) Mary and Joseph traveled with their donkey. Many other people were traveling too. When they reached Bethlehem, it was so crowded, Joseph and Mary could not find a place to stay. Every house was full.

(Page 4) Then they found a barn to use. Joseph made a bed with straw and a blanket. Mary said, "I think the baby will be born tonight, in this barn."

"God will watch over us," Joseph said.

And Baby Jesus was born that very night!

(Page 5) Nearby, shepherds were watching over their sheep. Because God wanted others to know that this special baby had been born, angels appeared to tell the shepherds.

"We must go see the baby," the shepherds said, and they did.

(Page 6) Another way God told people about Jesus was through a bright star in the sky. Some wise men understood it was a sign that a special child had been born. They followed the star so they could visit Jesus. When they reached him, they bowed down and gave him gifts. Mary smiled and cuddled her special baby.

(Page 7, back cover)

Christmas Peace

In Iraq, Christmas Day church services are concluded with a beautiful custom. The bishop blesses several people with a touch, such as on the shoulder. That person in turn touches the person next to him or her, who touches the next one, and so on. Each person receives and gives the "touch of peace" on Christmas Day. This is an easy yet meaningful ritual that can be done with family members and friends.

A Christmas Legend

This story is told at Christmas time in the Netherlands. Read the story out loud and then invite the children to help you retell the story by acting it out.

Story: The Three Skaters

Much of the Netherlands is covered with water, and in the winter, when this water is covered with ice, people can skate from place to place. One cold Christmas Eve, many years ago, a farmer was skating towards home with a nearly empty sack slung over his shoulder. There had been a poor harvest that year, and the farmer had only a few apples to bring home to his family for their Christmas dinner. Soon he was joined by a neighbor, a miller, who carried just a few loaves of bread in a sack for his family. It was all he had for his family. Both men were sad and did not speak. Only the sounds of their skates scraping the ice was heard in the cold air. Soon another neighbor joined them, who had nothing but a bit of bacon in a sack for his family's Christmas. They skated on in silence.

Then, in the still night, they heard a baby's cry. Startled, the three neighbors looked at one another. There was nothing in sight except an old, unused barn. They heard the cry again. "No one has been near that barn in years," said the farmer.

"Perhaps someone needs help," said the miller.

The three men skated to the shore and hurried to the rickety barn. Inside they found a young woman with a newborn baby. A man was with them, trying to gather enough of the scattered hay to make a place for them to sleep. "We have traveled a long way and need to stop," the man explained. "We won't stay here long."

It was cold in the barn. The three men noticed there was no food in sight. The farmer opened his sack and gave the young woman his few apples. The miller gave his bread, and third neighbor contributed the bacon.

"Thank you! Oh, thank you!" the woman said, holding her baby close to keep him warm.

All three men smiled. "Beautiful baby," the farmer said, and then the men left the barn.

Back on the ice, they skated together, wondering and worrying about the poor and cold family they had seen. But soon each man set off separately towards his home. As each one trudged through the snow to his house, he noticed that the empty sack on his back felt heavy again. The closer he got to home, the heavier the sack became. By the time each man opened his door, the sack was so heavy, he could hardly carry it!

In all three homes that night, the heavy sacks were spilled out. Food of all kinds fell out—breads, cakes, fruits, meats and candy! What a feast! As the children and mothers exclaimed and delighted over the bounty, the fathers silently marveled at the miracle they had experienced that night.

Discussion Starter: What was the miracle?

December 26 – St. Stephen

St. Stephen was chosen to be a deacon to the apostles. His job was to distribute money to poor Christians. To honor his faithful service to others, and because his feast day comes in the Christmas season, there is a custom of saving money during Advent and donating it on his feast day to those in need.

Activity: *Collect Pennies*

On this day invite the children to bring their pennies in. Collect the pennies in a big glass jar near your celebration or prayer corner. At the end of the day suggest two places where the children's money could be donated. Ask the children for their input.

December 27 – St. John the Evangelist and Apostle

St. John and his brother St. James were two of the first men called to be Jesus' apostles. They were fishermen from Galilee. John was with Jesus for many important events, such as the Transfiguration and the agony in the garden. John is described as resting his head on Jesus' chest during the Last Supper, and is the only apostle that was present at the foot of the cross.

Activity: *Fishers of Others*

After explaining to the children that Jesus called St. John to become a fisherman of people, remind the children that we too are to spread the Good News. On multicolored sheets of tag-board, have the children make a fish by tracing their hands with all of their fingers closed together. Cut the fish out and decorate them with markers and glitter. Use a paper punch and ribbon to finish this delightful fish ornament, reminding the children that Christmas is a perfect time to spread the word about God's love!

December 28 – The Holy Innocents

"Once Herod realized that he had been deceived by the astrologers he became furious. He ordered the massacre of all boys two years old and younger in Bethlehem." Matthew 2:16

Following the birth of Jesus, King Herod was very threatened by the possibility that a new king had been born. He ordered all baby boys under the age of 2 years old to be killed. It is thought that this massacre went on for two years. Because Bethlehem was such a small town, modern historians believe that fifteen to twenty babies were killed during this time. The Church has referred to these babies as the first martyrs of Christ and hence the observance of this day. While this is not a story that you would share with young children, you can take this opportunity to celebrate human life!

Prayer

On this day, dear Lord, we pray for the lives of all babies. We pray that they be well taken care of and loved. In Jesus' name we pray. Amen.

Activity: *Baby Collection*

Think about how you can help babies in your community. Invite families to donate baby clothes, diapers and food to be given to a center that helps struggling parents.

1st Sunday After Christmas – The Holy Family

"They made haste and found Mary and Joseph and the baby lying in the manger." Luke 2:16

The feast of the Holy Family is celebrated on the first Sunday after Christmas. It is dedicated to Jesus, Mary and Joseph and their life together as a family. The Feast of the Holy Family was officially recognized as a feast day in 1921.

Prayer

Today we celebrate the lives of the holy family, Jesus, Mary and Joseph. We are thankful for our own moms, dads, sisters, brothers, grandparents, cousins, aunts and uncles. How lucky we are to have so many people in our lives that care about us. Help us to grow strong in the ties that bring us together and our love for one another. Amen.

Activities

Holy Family Discussion

Talk about the family of Mary, Joseph and Jesus. Did Jesus learn some of the same things from his parents that you learn from your parents? Did he ever get into trouble? Joseph was a carpenter; did he teach Jesus how to be one too? Who do you suppose taught Jesus to pray?

Our Special Families

Have the children name the members of their families. What is special about your family? Is anyone named after someone in your family?

Family Dolls

Make a family of paper dolls and have the children color each family member and with adult help add their names. To make paper dolls cut a strip of paper 20" by 5." Fold the paper every 4" as you would if you were making a paper fan. Draw a simple figure like the one below on the folded paper making sure the arms are on the folded edge. Cut out the tracing while still folded. Open up the dolls and color.

December

Family Dolls

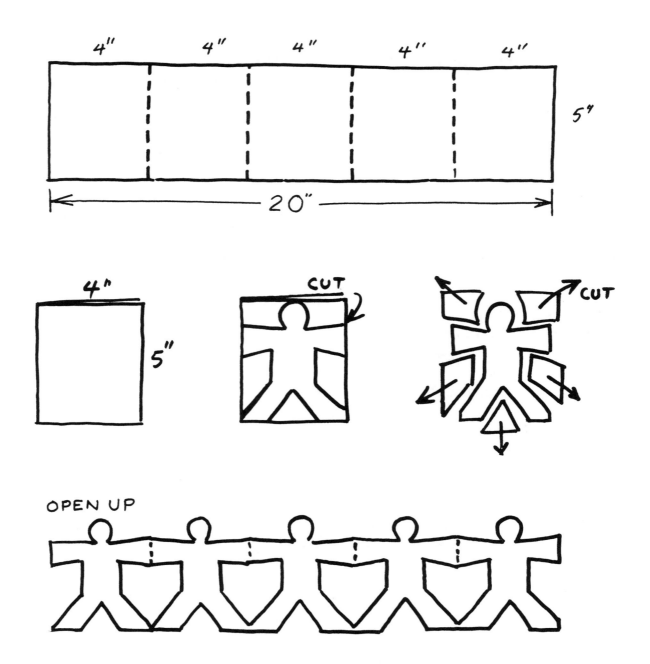

January at a Glance

Dedication for January: The Holy Childhood of Jesus
January's Liturgical Color
Patron Saints of the Month
January 1: New Year's Day
New Year's Day Celebration
January 1: Solemnity of Mary
January 4: St. Elizabeth Ann Seton
January 6: Epiphany and Celebration Table Ideas
Sunday Following Epiphany: Baptism of the Lord
Celebrated on the 3rd Monday in January: Martin Luther King Day
January 17: St. Anthony of Egypt
January 21: St. Agnes
January 27: St. Angela Merici
January 28: St. Thomas Aquinas
January 31: St. John Bosco

Dedication for January: The Holy Childhood of Jesus

This month we remember the years Jesus spent growing up with Mary and Joseph.

January's Liturgical Color

Ordinary Time: Green

Green is the color of hope and life.

Patron Saints of the Month

January 17: Anthony of Egypt: basketmakers, butchers
January 24: Francis de Sales: authors, journalists, deafness
January 28: Thomas Aquinas: students, schools
January 31: John Bosco: editors, young people, laborers

January 1 – New Year's Day

January is the first day of the year for most countries in the world. It is a day to look back at the year and to celebrate happy times. On this day we also look ahead to new beginnings, hopes and dreams for the future.

January

January 1 has not always been the first day of the New Year. At one time, the Romans celebrated March 1 as the beginning of the year. During the Middle Ages people celebrated the first day of the year on March 25. On this day they celebrated the Annunciation of our Lord, (the day the angel Gabriel visited Mary to tell her that she would be the mother of Jesus). This changed in the 1600's when many nations changed to the Gregorian calendar, which is the one used today. In 1752 the United States officially adopted the Gregorian calendar and January 1 as New Year's Day.

Prayer for New Year's Day

As we celebrate New Year's Day, let's take some time to think about all of the blessings of the past year. What blessings from God did we receive and what challenges did we face? Lord, we are grateful for the many good things this past year brought us. Thank you for the gifts of health, family and friends. Be with us as we begin this new year of_____ (add the year). As we grow closer to you, help us to learn from the difficult days and be thankful for the good days. In Jesus' name we pray. Amen.

Activities
New Year's Discussion

Discuss New Year's celebrations the children may have had with their families. What were their favorites? Ask them about New Year's Resolutions. Share with each other some of the things you would like to change about yourselves or work on in the year ahead.

Bible Verse Custom

Colonial Americans had a New Year's custom of randomly opening the Bible, pointing to a verse and then reflecting on that verse throughout the year. Older children will enjoy this custom. For younger children choose a few age-appropriate Bible verses and write them on heavy paper. Place the Bible verses in a fish bowl or hat. Have each child take a verse and share it with the others. Everyone takes his or her verse home to put in a special place to ponder as the year goes on. Send parents a brief note explaining the Bible custom and making suggestions for follow through at home.

Pineapple Welcome

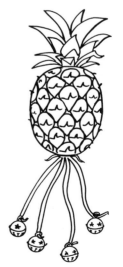

The pineapple has long been a symbol of welcome for Americans. Purchase a whole pineapple for your prayer table as a sign of welcome in the New Year. To add to this tradition write a blessing or a short prayer for each child on an 18" length of white ribbon with gold marker. Tie a gold jingle bell to one end of the ribbon and place the other end of the ribbon under the pineapple. After sharing your New Year Prayer, have the children take turns pulling one ribbon from the pineapple. Read each child's blessing or prayer to the rest of the class. Have the children take home their New Year's blessing and encourage them to put it in a special place for the days ahead.

Pinecone Pineapples

To make individual pineapples gather enough short, round pinecones for each child in the class. Place the pinecone on its bottom and tape a green piece of gathered tissue paper about 2" by 6" to the top of it. Add a brief explanation of the pinecone symbol and add the New Year's prayer.

New Year's Day Celebration

While most New Year celebrations are secular, you can recognize that this is a sacred day. Serve a special "Blessings Cake." Have each family member say a prayer of thanksgiving for something in the past year. Then add small candles to the cake to symbolize each prayer. After the thanksgiving prayers have been said, light the candles and ask God for blessings on this coming year. Then, wish everyone a happy New Year, blow out the candles, and enjoy the cake.

January 1 – Solemnity of Mary

Upon arriving the angel said to her, "Rejoice O highly favored daughter! The Lord is with you. Blessed are you among women." Luke 1:28

The Solemnity of Mary is observed on January 1 and is a holy day of obligation. This day is the major feast day of Mary. We treasure the life and contributions Mary made to the life of Jesus and the Church. We honor her as a faithful servant of God and Mother of Jesus.

Prayer

Holy Mary, Mother of God, we ask you to pray for us this day. What an example of faithfulness you are to us. Without hesitating you said yes to God when the angel Gabriel told you that you would have a son who should be named Jesus, who would be born to you by the power of the Holy Spirit. We pray that as we grow in faith we too will say yes to God. In Jesus' name we pray. Amen.

Activities

Mary's Prayer

Pray the Hail Mary with the children.
Hail Mary, full of grace, the Lord is with you.
Blessed are you among women and blessed is the fruit of your womb, Jesus.
Holy Mary, Mother of God, pray for us sinners now and at the hour of our death. Amen.

Mary Discussion

Talk about the kind of woman Mary was. Was she prayerful? What kinds of things did she teach Jesus? Look at some paintings that illustrate Mary. How did artists see her?

Flowers for Mary

Place flowers in your prayer center as a reminder of this special day to remember Mary.

Altar Visit

If your church has an altar dedicated to Mary, visit it, light a candle and share one of the above prayers.

White Ribbons

Tie a white ribbon around the wrist of each child as a reminder of this special day to honor Mary.

Hail Mary Prayer Card

Use the pattern below to make a prayer card with the Hail Mary to send home. Enlarge and trace the pattern below on brightly colored construction paper. Have the children draw Mary's face in the rounded top of the pattern. Glue a paper card, with the Hail Mary printed on it, to the center as shown. Fold the sides toward the center; they will overlap. Decorate the front and back of the prayer card with stickers.

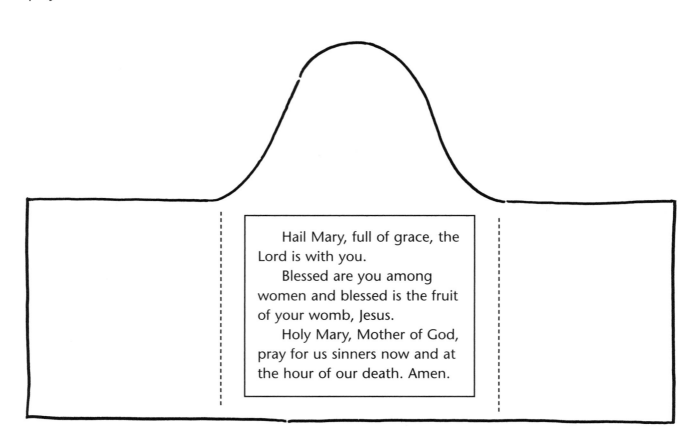

Hail Mary, full of grace, the Lord is with you.

Blessed are you among women and blessed is the fruit of your womb, Jesus.

Holy Mary, Mother of God, pray for us sinners now and at the hour of our death. Amen.

January 4 – St. Elizabeth Ann Seton

Elizabeth Seton was the first person born in the United States to be declared a saint, but she was not born to a Catholic family. Her stepmother taught her to pray and read Scripture, and her father taught her to love and serve the poor. These lessons stayed with her as her life brought her much upheaval and change. Wealthy and happily married at age nineteen, Elizabeth was widowed and penniless, with five children, within a few years. She turned to God, and found she was being called to join the Catholic Church. She dedicated her life to serving God. In addition to raising her own children, she opened the first American Catholic school, started an orphanage, and founded a religious order of women, the Daughters of Charity.

Discussion Starter: What were some of the things that Elizabeth Ann Seton did?

January 6 – Epiphany

(Or the first Sunday following the Feast of the Holy Family, or the twelfth day after Christmas)

"When they saw the star, they rejoiced exceedingly with great joy; and going into the house they saw the child with Mary his mother, and they fell down and worshiped him. Then, opening their treasures, they offered him gifts, gold and frankincense and myrrh. And being warned in a dream not to return to Herod, they departed to their own country by another way." Matthew 2:10-12

The roots of our modern day Epiphany are many. The word itself comes from a Greek word that means, "appearance" or "to show oneself." On this day Christians originally celebrated God becoming man at the Baptism of Jesus. Today eastern churches still celebrate this day as the Baptism of our Lord. In the Catholic tradition we observe Epiphany as the day the three kings visited Jesus and acknowledged Him as the savior the world had been waiting for.

Tradition gives them the names Melchoir, Balthazar and Casper. We know that they were scientists who studied astronomy, math and probably medicine. They were aware of the prophecies of the birth of God's Son and the salvation that He would bring to the world. They looked for a sign of the Messiah's birth in the stars. When the brightest star they had ever seen appeared in the sky, the kings knew that they had to follow it to find the Son of God.

Prayer for Epiphany

A bright star guided the three kings to the place where Jesus was born. The kings were very happy to see the new baby and they gave him gifts of frankincense, gold and myrrh. On this Epiphany day, we are thankful for the gift God gave us, his Son, Jesus. We are also thankful for the gifts we received and were able to give to others this holiday season. We ask that in the days ahead, we remember others and continue the spirit of giving all year long. Amen.

Activities
Door Markings

Encourage families to bless their homes by writing (with chalk) the year with the initials of the kings on the top of the doors like this: 20+C+M+B+03 (The first and last two numbers reflect the current year). In a zippered bag, send home instructions, with a piece of colored chalk and the following prayer:

Lord Jesus, we ask that you bless our home today. We thank you for the love we have for each other and for you. With the prayers of the saints, Casper, Melchior and Balthasar, we ask that our home be a place of happiness, love, understanding, acceptance and safety for all who enter. As we write our New Year and the initials of the Three Wise Kings on our door, we pray in your name. Amen.

Three Kings Images

Look through your box of used Christmas cards, taking out the ones with pictures of the three kings. Post these in your prayer corner or add them to a bulletin board titled, "Following the Star" or "Searching for Jesus."

Kings Cake

Share a Kings Cake with the children in your class. Hide a candy coin in one or more cupcakes. The child who gets the coin in their cake is king for the day. Present the king with a crown and little gift.

Celebration Table

The three kings, or the magi, tell us that all peoples are welcomed by Jesus. They also encourage us to travel far, in our hearts and minds, to come to Jesus. To symbolize this, cover the table with dark blue fabric, place unbreakable magi statues on one side of the table, and a figure of the Christ Child on the other. Make paper stars, and lay them on the table in a path between them, so the men are following the star path.

Star Ribbons

Trace three stars on heavy paper. With glitter pens write the words: Joy, Hope, and Peace on each of the stars. Staple the stars on a piece of ribbon and make a loop at the top for hanging.

Follow the Star Game

Play Follow the Star game. Cover a cardboard star with aluminum foil. Have the children cover their eyes while someone hides the star in your classroom. Everyone looks for the star and the person who finds it first hides it for the next round of the game.

Show and Tell

Plan a special Show and Tell for the week after Christmas. Everyone is invited to bring in a favorite toy. Use the following blessing of toys with the whole group.

Prayer

Dear God, thank you for the gift of your Son, Jesus, at Christmas. We also thank you for the blessing of family and friends with whom we celebrated this special time. Today as we share the gifts that we received in your honor,

we ask for your blessing. (At this time move around the circle and touch each child gently on the head and ask for God's blessing.) "God bless Sarah and her new panda bear" or "God bless Michael and his new football."

Sunday Following Epiphany – Baptism of the Lord

Jesus came from Galilee to be baptized by John the Baptist. After Jesus was baptized he came out of the water and the sky opened and he saw the Spirit of God descend like a dove and hover over him. With that a voice from the heavens said, "This is my beloved Son with whom I am well pleased." Matthew 3: 13-17

This feast is dedicated to the Baptism of Jesus by John the Baptist. Jesus was an adult when his cousin John baptized him in the Jordan River. The Baptism of Jesus marked the beginning of his public ministry.

Prayer

Just as Jesus was baptized with water into the family of God by his cousin John, we too have been baptized with water into our community of faith. Today we are grateful for the new life we have in Jesus through our baptism. Help us to live every day as children of God. Amen.

Activities
Blessings

Pass around a clear bowl of water after the baptism prayer above. Have the children dip their fingers into the water and make the Sign of the Cross. Or bless children by making the Sign of the Cross on their foreheads with holy water.

Baptism Discussion

Talk about the rite of baptism. If possible watch a baptism in your community.

Model Baptism

Do a model baptism with the children using a baby doll and inviting your pastor or another teacher to be the celebrant.

Photos at the Font

Take a photo of each child at the baptismal font of your church.

Baptism Celebrations

Find out the date of each child's baptism and celebrate it with the class using the blessing above. Also have the children bring in pictures of their own baptisms.

Shell Remembrances

The scalloped seashell is one of the symbols of baptism. Ask your community for donations of seashells and use them to make remembrances of baptism for the children in your group. Lace a ribbon through a hole in the shell. (If there is not a hole in the shell, use hot glue to fasten it to a ribbon or ask a volunteer to drill holes in the shells.) Make a necklace with the seashell or use a shorter ribbon to make it an ornament. With a gold fine point pen, write the name of the child and the date of his/her baptism on the inside of the shell.

Celebrated on the 3rd Monday in January – Martin Luther King Day

"I have a dream that one day this nation will rise up and live the true meaning of its creed: 'We hold these truths to be self-evident that all men are created equal.' I have a dream that my four little children will one day live in a nation where they will not be judged by the color of their skin, but by the content of their character." (Excerpt from a speech give by Martin Luther King on August 28,1963 at the Lincoln Memorial in Washington, D.C.)

Martin Luther King, Jr. was the leader of the civil rights movement of the 1950s and 1960s in America. He was a Baptist minister and excellent speaker who inspired others. Martin Luther King worked for integration, equal rights for all under the law and promoted peaceful demonstrations to increase the awareness of the injustices in the U.S. for people of color. In 1964 King won the Nobel Peace Prize for his work. Martin Luther King and George Washington are the only two Americans in history to have their birthdays named as national holidays.

Prayer

Today we honor Martin Luther King, a man who loved God very much. Dr. King dreamed of love, peace and justice. He dreamed that we could all work together and live in peace no matter what the color of our skin. As we remember Dr. King's birthday today, we are thankful for the many things he did for the people of our country. We ask God to help us to love one another, always work together and live in peace. Amen.

Dr. King and Jesus

For Christian children, it is also important to tie Dr. King's work in with the words of Jesus. Dr. King studied theology deeply and incorporated a great deal of spirituality into his work. With the story "Martin Follows Jesus," you can help children see how Dr. King followed one teaching of Jesus in particular.

Story: Martin Follows Jesus

One day, when Jesus was on the mountainside teaching many people, he said, "Remember a time when you were so hungry that you couldn't think of anything but eating. You didn't want to play or sleep, or do anything but eat. You were longing for food. God wants you to have that same kind of longing for what is right. God wants you to work so that there is more good than bad in the world. You must long for all people to be treated fairly. Blessed are those who long for what is fair."

Two thousand years after Jesus said this, a little boy named Martin Luther King, Jr. was growing up in the United States. He had a best friend. They rode bikes and played baseball and football together. When it was time to start school, however, Martin went to a school just for black children, and his friend went to a school just for white children.

When Martin came home from school that first day, he went over to his friend's house and knocked on the door as usual. The mother came out and told Martin her son was too busy to play today. And he would be too busy tomorrow, too, and the day after that. Martin should not come back to play — ever.

Sad and confused, Martin went home. His mother took him onto her lap and explained that some white people did not want their children to play with black children. This was unfair! Martin knew that skin color should not make any difference, and his mother agreed. "You are as good as anyone," she said. And Martin knew, too, that God loved him.

Martin saw many more unfair things: in his town, there were signs saying that only white people could use certain water fountains. White people and black people could not sit near each other in theaters or restaurants, on trains or buses. He saw other things as well. He watched as his father worked so black teachers would get paid as much as white teachers. He saw his parents hungering for what was fair, just as Jesus had taught.

One day, Martin's father took him to get new shoes. A sign in the store said the black people could only sit in the back of the store. Martin's father ignored that sign, and he and Martin went to the front, waiting for a clerk to come with shoes for Martin to try on. But instead, the clerk told them to move to the back of the store. Martin's father said, "We will buy shoes right here, or we will not buy shoes at this store at all." He and Martin left the store without any new shoes.

All through his childhood, Martin lived under such unfairness. It was a much bigger problem than just the shoe store. He learned how badly black people were treated in other cities. But his parents were showing him that he was a good and important person, and he was taught that Jesus thought so too.

Martin also saw and read about people who were working to make changes in the unfairness. He prayed and he studied. He longed to make changes, too. He wanted all black Americans to be proud of who they were. Martin longed for what was fair.

Martin spent his life working for this. Because of his work, prayers and leadership, the laws keeping black and white people apart were changed. He taught others how to change unfair laws that kept black people from voting. Because of Martin's hunger and thirst for what was right, many people in our country today are working to have good schools, safe neighborhoods, and good jobs for all people. Still, there is more work to do. We all must hunger and thirst and work for what is right.

Activities

People Terms

The terms "black" and "white" are used in this story because most young children will quickly understand them. However, take this opportunity to talk about various ways of labeling people as well as the multi-culturalism of the United States. Explain that in our country, most people came from somewhere else. Some just recently arrived, and for others it is their grandparents, or even great, great, great grandparents who came here a long time ago. While it is always best to look at each person as an individual, and not at which groups he or she might belong to, sometimes we have to use names for groups. Introduce this intriguing way of choosing names: look at a world map, pointing out areas such as Asia, Europe, etc. Use this information then to make respectful names. Explain terms such as African-American, European-American, Asian-American, and for the people who came here first, Native-American.

Unfair Rules

Even young children understand the issue of unfairness. At snack time, propose an unfair classroom rule, such as only children with red shoes can play in the gym. Ask children how they would feel if you really had that rule. Why is it unfair?

Exposure to Multicultures

Perhaps one of the best ways teachers can promote racial justice is by helping all children become comfortable with differences. Regularly bring in picture books that show multi-ethnic children playing and working together. Prejudice need not be the topic of the story. Invite adults of a variety of ethnic backgrounds to come in from time to time, just to read stories, enjoy snack with your class, etc.

Paper Dolls

Use the paper doll pattern provided and have the children make dolls to represent themselves. Make sure your crayons offer a wide choice of skin tones. Display these on a bulletin board or in your prayer corner. Add the words, "Love One Another" or "Dream the Dream."

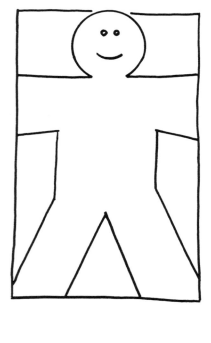

People Pins

Use puzzle pieces from an old puzzle to make people pins. Paint the pieces that look like the shape of a person with paints of various skin tones, add facial features, and glue a jewelry pin to the back. Write the words, "God (heart) all children," on the front of the pin. Have the children wear these for your prayer today.

Rainbow Mural

Make a rainbow mural using the hand cutouts of all of the children in the program. Have each child trace and then cut out her or his handprint. Use the colors red, orange, yellow, green and blue. Have the children write a prayer for peace on their hands. Tape the hands in a half circle to make a rainbow. Title the bulletin board "God loves all children."

January 17 – St. Anthony of Egypt

Anthony lived a few hundred years after Jesus did. He grew up in a wealthy family. One day, when he was a young man, he was at church and listened to the Gospel. In it, Jesus said, "Go and sell all you own and give the money to those who are poor." Anthony thought those words fit him perfectly. He did just that, and he walked out into the desert. There he lived for years all by himself, praying, studying and working in his garden. He became so holy, people said his face had a beautiful light about it. After many years of being alone, Anthony started to teach others about loving God. A few times he went back to cities to work, but always felt God calling him back to live alone.

Anthony lived until he was 105 years old. In his last years, he had pets. In Mexico, and in some Central American countries, children celebrate Anthony's feast day by painting stripes or polka dots on cows and sheep! They decorate their chickens and cats with flowers and put clothing on them! Then they bring their animals to church for a blessing.

Discussion Starter: What was the Gospel message that fit St. Anthony perfectly?

January 21 – St. Agnes

St. Agnes was a thirteen-year-old martyr who died around 258. As her feast day comes in the winter, some people used to refer to snowflakes as "St. Agnes flowers." Cut out paper snowflakes on this day and hang them in windows.

Activity: *St. Agnes Flowers*

Make frosty painted snowflakes. Mix 1 cup powdered white tempera paint and 2 tablespoons wallpaper paste. Add approximately 1/2 cup liquid laundry starch and mix until the paint is stiff as frosting. Use a stubby paintbrush or a craft stick to apply the paint to paper, cardboard or glass.

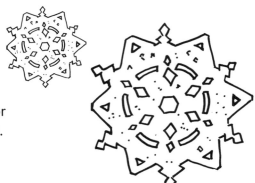

January 27 – St. Angela Merici

As a young woman, Angela was upset when she saw that poor children were not taught classes about Jesus and praying. She set up classes and spent years teaching. Other women became interested in her work, and Angela organized them into a religious community. She created the first teaching order of women.

Activity: *Bandanna Neck Scarves*

Make fun bandanna neck scarves for another class that will be sure to spread God's love all around. Cut bandannas in half, from corner to corner. On the right side of the scarf, print, "Jesus (heart) you!" with puffy paint. Younger children who cannot print the message can add decorative hearts.

January 28 – St. Thomas Aquinas

Thomas was a very quiet student. Some of the other students thought that he was stupid because he didn't talk in class. But they were completely wrong! Thomas was brilliant and became a very important teacher and writer. He wrote about God and Jesus, and about what is true in life and what is not. Thomas loved God very much. He studied, taught and wrote all because of God.

Discussion Starter: Thomas had the gifts of teaching and writing. What are some examples of other talents or gifts people you know have been blessed with?

January 31 – St. John Bosco

John Bosco grew up on a small farm in Italy with his brothers. His father died when John was only two, and though his mother worked hard, they were very poor. But John was rich in other ways: he was smart, funny and loving; he was a good writer, and he had an incredible memory; he could juggle and walk on a tightrope; he had lots of energy, and he could work hard. And, he knew God wanted him to become a priest and help children. Off he went to school, wearing hand-me-down clothes, and working many jobs to stay there. Soon he began working with children. At that time, there were many children who left their poor families on farms in hopes of getting jobs in a city. Most did not. They were hungry, scared and homeless. John invited these children on picnics, where he walked a tightrope or did handstands to make them laugh. He gave them good food and played ball with them. He taught them about Jesus and he prayed with them. Soon John found buildings for these children to live in. With his own mother's help, he fed them, cut their hair, found them jobs, taught them to read, write, do math, sing, to become clever thinkers, to pray and trust in God. With his great energy and with a smile on his face, St. John Bosco helped thousands of children.

Here is a story about a very special friend who helped John Bosco.

Story: The Saint and His Big, Ugly Dog

There were many people who saw the work Fr. John Bosco was doing and frowned. For several reasons, they wished he would give up working with all those homeless kids. Perhaps, some of these people thought, they could "convince" the priest to give up.

So they made plans to scare and even hurt John. He was now often in danger as he went about doing his work.

One day, a dog showed up at John's house. It was huge and gray, and frightening to look at, a big hulk of a dog. No one knew where it had come from. Nobody had seen it before. But it seemed to love Fr. John and went with him everywhere.

With Grigio, as the dog was called, at John's side, no one dared attack him. Anyone foolish enough to try was soon scared off by Grigio. This happened many times.

One day, Fr. John and his dog were inside a building. When it was time to leave, Grigio growled at John. John cautiously walked towards the door, but Grigio snarled and showed his teeth. The huge dog blocked the door, and John was trapped. John was puzzled, and he did not try to get closer to the well-guarded door. Why was Grigio, always so loving, suddenly acting so strangely?

After a few hours, Grigio finally relaxed. He stopped growling and moved away from the door. John went on his way. Later, he found out that right outside, several men had been hiding, waiting to hurt John when he came outside. Grigio had kept John indoors until they left and it was safe again for John.

John continued his work, helping more and more children and Grigio continued to protect him. Eventually, the people who were against him changed their minds. All the danger was gone now. One evening, Grigio showed up as usual. He rubbed his head against John and held up one huge paw. Then the dog wandered off into the nighttime darkness, and never came back.

Discussion Starter: How did John Bosco help children? Why did John Bosco need Grigio's help?

January

Activity: *Sign Reminders*

Cut out large street-sign shapes out of tagboard, one per child. Have the children use markers or paints to draw something on each sign that God gave us to help others. Display in the hallways.

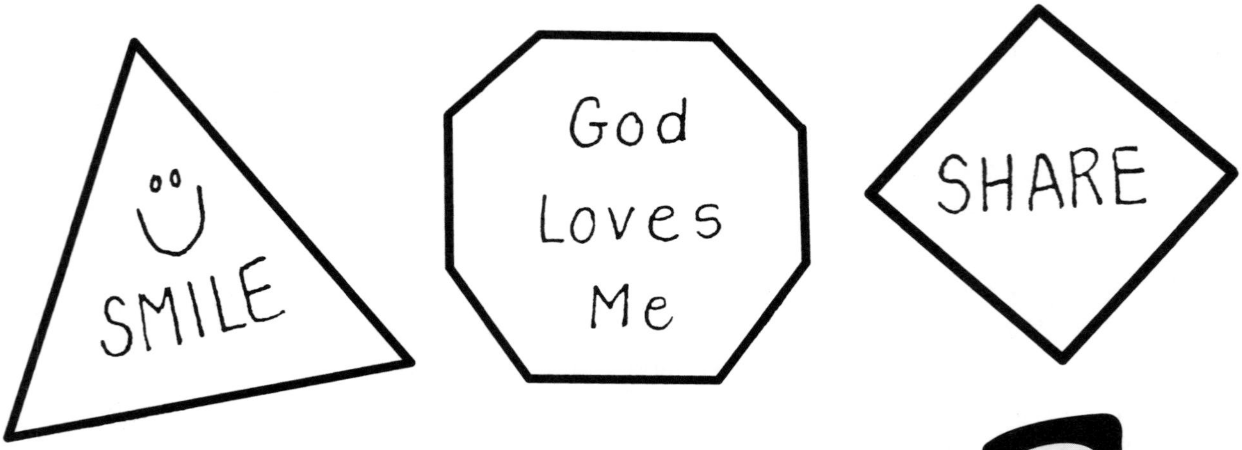

SMILE

God Loves Me

SHARE

Project Checklist

February at a Glance

Dedication of the Month: The Holy Family

February's Liturgical Color

Patron Saints of the Month

February 1: St. Brigid of Ireland

February 2: The Presentation of the Lord and Candlemas Day

February 3: St. Blaise

February 6: St. Paul Miki and Companions

February 11: Our Lady of Lourdes

February 14: St. Valentine's Day and Celebration Table Ideas

Celebrated the 3rd Monday in February: Presidents Day

February 18: Blessed Fra Angelico

Dedication for February: The Holy Family

The Holy Family is made up of Jesus, Mary and Joseph. They are our best examples of love, charity, hope, and fidelity.

February's Liturgical Colors

Ordinary Time: Green

Green is the color of hope and life.

Lent: Purple

Purple is used during Lent to symbolize penance and sacrifice.

Patron Saints of the Month

February 1: Brigid: Ireland, dairy workers, scholars

February 3: Blaise: those with sore throats, diseases of the throat

February 3: Ansgar: Denmark

February 5: Agatha: nurses, single women

February 8: Jerome Emiliani: orphans

February 10: Scholastica: children with conditions such as cerebral palsy

February 1 – St. Brigid of Ireland

Brigid is one of the best-loved saints of Ireland. She lived a very long time ago, but there are still many stories about her. When she was a child, she was a servant in a house. She understood that Jesus wanted people to help one another. Brigid felt she must help everyone who needed food or other things. So, she gave away milk, eggs, bread, cheese—anything she could find, she gave to hungry people. Over and over again, she was told not to do that, but Brigid, knowing Jesus was right, kept on helping others. Finally, when she was a young woman, the people she worked for told her to leave. They gave up trying to change her, and they were tired of having their food given away. Happily, Brigid left that life behind and became a sister. Eventually, she became the head of a very large monastery, where both sisters and monks worked and prayed. It became an important place of learning. Brigid was greatly respected by both men and women. She served God and she served people in many ways. It is said, that sometimes, she drove around in a chariot!

The monastery that Brigid began and ran was called *Cil dara*, or "church of the oak." Some of the work done there was the making of Bibles. Because there were no machines to print yet, each page was written by hand, in beautiful letters. The pages were also decorated in lovely colors, with drawings of angels, eagles, lions, and other symbols. These are called "illuminated manuscripts." These were so extraordinary that some people claimed that only angels could have made them.

Story: Sister Brigid Serves Dinner

Young Sister Brigid and seven other women lived together in a convent. They worked hard, raising cows and chickens, planting and harvesting fruit trees and gardens. With these, they prepared food and fed all the hungry people who came to them.

One day, many hungry people had come to the convent. All the eggs were scrambled; the butter had been used up on the bread, which was gone, too. Not a pear remained in the bowls. Not a drop of milk remained in the pitchers.

Then before the good sisters had time to relax, word came that they were to receive more visitors—seven bishops!

The sisters were very upset. "What can we do? There is no food left in the house to serve them!" one of the women wailed.

Of course, there were no supermarkets or restaurants, either.

Brigid smiled. "I think God will provide this meal," she said. "Go ask the hens if they might be so kind as to give us more eggs. Then talk with the cows. Perhaps they will give us a bit more milk. Oh, and go ask the fruit trees to ripen some fruit."

As the other sisters left the room, Brigid stirred up the fire of the oven. Then she opened the oven door and smiled again. There were two loaves of hot, golden-brown bread!

Soon the others returned. One carried a pitcher filled with fresh milk. Another carried a basket filled with hens' eggs. Two others held their aprons out, which were filled with pears.

"Time to cook!" Brigid said cheerfully. "God has blessed us again!"

February 2 – Presentation of the Lord and Candlemas Day

Simeon took baby Jesus in his arms and said these words, "Now, Master, you can dismiss your servant in peace, you have fulfilled your word. For my eyes have witnessed your saving deed displayed for all to see. A revealing light to the Gentile, the glory of your people Israel." Luke 2:29-30

The Presentation of the Lord is the story of Jesus being brought to the temple in Jerusalem. According to Jewish law a woman whose firstborn was a son was to stay in seclusion for forty days after giving birth. Parents then brought their children (after forty days) to the temple to be blessed. Mary and Joseph brought Jesus to the temple in Jerusalem. The highlight of this visit to the temple was meeting Simeon, who was a very devout Jew. Simeon had prayed that he would not die without seeing the Messiah. As Mary and Joseph arrived at the temple Simeon was filled with the Spirit. He took Jesus in his arms, blessed him and proclaimed that this child was truly the Son of God.

Candlemas

The Feast of the Presentation is also called Candlemas or Candle Mass Day. Since the seventh century, there has been a tradition of blessing candles before Mass that day and giving them to people. These blessed candles would be used in the year ahead, for Masses, baptisms, weddings, and in the home, too. This feast day was probably chosen for this tradition because it symbolizes that Christ is the Light of the World. In some parishes, people carry lighted candles around the church and out into the nearby streets, to show that we carry the Light of Christ to everyone in the world.

Prayer

Jesus, you are the Light of the World. We know that you are the Good News of love and hope in our lives. We know that your light and love will get us through any difficult and dark times. Be with us. In your name we pray. Amen.

Activities

Song

Sing, "This Little Light of Mine" and light a candle when you pray today.

Candle Blessing

Make arrangements with your pastor to bless the candles your church uses. Use the prayer above and add the line, "Bless these candles, dear Lord, that they may shine long and bright, reminding us of your presence and the light you bring to our lives."

Take-Home Candles

Make paper candles with the children to take home as a reminder of this special day. Cover toilet tissue tubes with colored paper or aluminum foil. Glue a paper flame to the top of the tube. Cut out a picture of baby Jesus from a used Christmas card picture (or use a sticker) and glue it to the center of the candle. Attach the prayer for this feast day and send home.

The Light of the World

On this feast day, speak with children about Jesus being called the Light of the World. Then light a large candle and read aloud the story of the Presentation. After that, light several smaller candles and place them in different corners of the room. Talk about how Jesus' light and love are now spread throughout the world.

More Candlemas and Groundhog Day Traditions:
The date of Candlemas is the same as Groundhog Day. Long before Groundhog Day, Candlemas Day as well as the feast of St. Brigid (February 1) were associated with the arrival of spring. Some English farmers believed that whatever the weather conditions were on Candlemas Day, the rest of the winter would be the opposite. A song was sung on this day:
"If Candlemas be fair and bright
Come, Winter, have another flight;
If Candlemas bring clouds and rain,
Go, Winter, and come not again."
(Taken from the Catholic Source Book)

German farmers believed that on the feast of Candlemas, the badger came out of hibernation. If it saw its shadow it would fearfully scurry back into the bed, and six more weeks of winter would result. Sound familiar? When some Germans emigrated to Pennsylvania, badgers were scarce, so they substituted the groundhog, also known as the woodchuck. It has only been about 100 years since the groundhog replaced the badger.

Activities
Weather Watch
Explain to children the old beliefs of Candlemas and Groundhog Day being indications of the weather to come. Talk about a farmer's need for predicting weather and how farmers of long ago did not have the scientific information they use today. On February 2, observe with the children what the weather conditions are, and record them on a calendar. Do this each day. Notice if the groundhog predicted correctly or incorrectly this year. Enjoy observing the small and large changes outside as winter gives way to spring. Encourage children to use descriptive words as they observe (e.g., that some branches are dark brown like coffee, others are a soft shade of green; describe the differences in texture of the snow on days with above and below freezing temperatures; observe buds on trees and note texture, size and color).

Flowers for the Nativity
Another connection between the end of winter and Candlemas is a folk belief that if the Christmas decorations stay up until Candlemas eve, the house would be haunted by troublesome goblins! Some people did leave their nativity sets up, placing fresh spring flowers at the manger for that day, to symbolize the coming of spring. Goblins or not, it would be lovely to bring in a bouquet of flowers for the feast of the Presentation.

February 3 – St. Blaise

St. Blaise was a good bishop who lived so long ago that we only know about him through stories. Some stories say that he was also a doctor, that he lived by himself, and he cured and tamed wild animals. Blaise lived at a time when many leaders did not want people to be Christians. Blaise was a good Christian who died because of his faith in Jesus.

Tradition

The most famous story about St. Blaise is that he cured a young boy who was choking on a fish bone. In the sixteenth century, a custom emerged from this story, the blessing of throats on the feast of St. Blaise. In some churches, unlit candles are tied into a cross shape and placed at a person's throat for a blessing. It is interesting that his feast day comes in February, when sore throats are common, and the day after Candlemas, candles are used for the blessing.

Activity: *Blaise's Blessings*

Tell children about St. Blaise. Then, placing your hands on a child's shoulders, say a simple blessing such as "St. Blaise, please ask God to watch over (name) in this season of colds and sore throats. Amen."

February 6 – St. Paul Miki and Companions

Paul Miki was a Japanese man who became a priest. He lived at a time when some people in the government of Japan did not want anyone to believe in Jesus. To stop this, they had many Christians killed. St. Paul Miki was one of them.

The people in the government then thought they had completely stopped Christianity in Japan. No missioners were allowed into the country. No one was heard saying Christian prayers. There were no churches or Christian festivals like Christmas. But 200 years later, much changed in the government, and Christian missioners were allowed to come into the country. Those missioners expected to have to start teaching people, but they found something else instead. Stories of Jesus, prayers such as the Our Father, and Jesus' teachings had been secretly taught by grandparents and parents to children, who then grew up and secretly told their children and grandchildren. This had been happening for 200 years! There were thousands of secret Japanese Christians!

Discussion Starter: What did the missionaries find when they were allowed back into Japan?

February 11 – Our Lady of Lourdes

About 150 years ago, Jesus' mother, Mary, appeared in a town called Lourdes, in France. Only one person saw her, a fourteen-year-old girl named Bernadette. Bernadette was very poor, and had great difficulty learning, but Mary had chosen her to tell people that they should care more about others, take care of one another, pray the rosary and not sin. She asked Bernadette to dig in the ground where Mary stood, and water bubbled up. A blind man was cured with the water. Now, each year, about two million people come to Lourdes, to pray, sing, and for some, to be cured by the water. There have been many cures.

Activity: *Image of Mary*

Bring in a good statue or painting of Our Lady of Lourdes. Tell the children that when Bernadette was asked about what Mary looked like, she said Mary didn't look like the statues in church, but was much more beautiful. Display the statue or picture. Together, say the Hail Mary.

February 14 – St. Valentine's Day

"... and the greatest of these is love." 1 Corinthians 13:13

According to Catholic history there were two martyred saints named Valentine. Little is known about either saint; however, there are legends about their lives and both have to do with the great love they had for God and others. St. Pope Gelasius I named February 14 as St. Valentine's Day in A.D. 496.

In A.D. 200 the emperor of Rome thought single men made better soldiers than married ones and he prohibited young men from marriage. According to one legend, St. Valentine secretly married couples.

The second St. Valentine was a very Christian man who was very good to the children in his town. When Valentine was imprisoned for refusing to worship the Roman gods, the children threw notes of love and good wishes through the bars of his jail cell. Legend also states that Valentine performed a miracle while in jail by restoring the sight of his jailer's daughter.

Prayer

On this Valentine's Day, we celebrate the love God has for us and the love we have for others. How lucky we are to have so much love in our lives! God of Love, we thank you today for the greatest gift of all, love. We thank you for our families, teachers and friends who have shown us how to love. Help us to remember on this Valentine's Day and everyday that love is the greatest gift we can give or receive. Amen.

Activities

The Gift of Love

Talk about how we share and show love to the people in our lives. Answer the question, "Who loves you?" Make a list of these people on a large paper heart and display it in your room.

Heart Hunt

Decorate your classroom with red heart cutouts. Tape them at the eye level of the children. Don't forget the bathroom, doors, cupboards, the backs and fronts of chairs and the floor. At the end of the day have a, "Heart Hunt" and give an extra treat to the child that collects the most paper hearts.

Face Hearts

With face crayons make a little heart on each child's cheek.

Valentines for the Needy

Add a little service project to your Valentine celebration. Collect red foods (foods that are red or that come in red packaging) for your local food pantry or send Valentine cards to the shut-ins of your community.

Celebration Table

Cover your table with a red cloth. Look for a picture of St. Valentine to put on the table. Have the children cut hearts and flowers out of white, pink and purple construction paper to adorn the top of the table. Then invite them to print the names of (or draw) people who love them on the hearts. Be sure to offer a prayer of thanksgiving for St. Valentine and all of the people who cover your Celebration Table with love!

Valentine Butterflies

Send blessings of love on Valentine butterflies. Cut four-inch hearts from heavy paper or wallpaper samples. Fold pipe cleaners in half, twist the wire half way to the top and spread the ends. Make a little bend on each end of the wire and glue to the center of the butterfly making sure the twisted end of the pipe cleaner is lined up to be the body of the butterfly. Fasten a Valentine message on the underside of the butterfly or use them to decorate a bulletin board or to give away.

Valentine Piñata

Make an easy piñata for your Valentine celebration. Fill a brown bag with wrapped candy and small toys. Gather the top together and tie it with a red ribbon. Have the children decorate the outside of the bag with leftover valentines or hearts they have made themselves. Tape strips of red, pink and white crepe paper to the bottom of the bag. Hang from a doorway, or basketball hoop. Blindfold each child as they take turns hitting the bag with a stick or plastic baseball bat.

Valentine Mobile

For a simple Valentine mobile, twist 3 pipe cleaners at the center and tie a ribbon for hanging also to the center. On the end of each pipe cleaner place two heart stickers back to back. Use these to decorate the room or send them home with a Valentine blessing.

February

Valentine Flowerpots

Make Valentine flowerpots to give to shut-ins in your neighborhood. Have the children paint 1" to 2" clay flowerpots with red or pink paint or use puffy paints to make designs. Place a ball of clay or small piece of Styrofoam in the bottom of the pot. Add a bit of shredded Mylar and place Valentine lollipops in the pot.

Celebrated the 3rd Monday in February – Presidents Day

Originally Presidents Day was set aside to honor George Washington's birthday, February 22. In recent times his birthday is celebrated on the third Monday of February. Most states have designated this day to honor all presidents.

Prayer

On this day we honor all presidents of the United States. We thank God for the willingness of these people to serve their country in so many ways. May God bless and keep our current president _____ (name of the current president) and all those who served before him. Amen.

Activities
Presidential Discussion

Talk about the job of the president. What does he do each day? What is the hardest part of his or her job? What would be the most fun part of the job?

Presidential Letters

Write to the president and express a concern regarding a specific issue or make your note one of thanksgiving.

Name of the President,
Honorable President of the United States of America
1600 Pennsylvania Avenue
Washington, DC 20500

Presidential Hats

Make a George Washington hat to honor the first president of the United States. For each hat, trace the hat and cut out three panels, coloring one red, one white and one blue. Staple the ends of the panels together to make the hat.

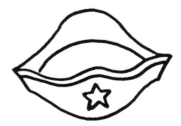

Money Art

Gather up pennies, nickels, quarters, and dimes and glue the heads of the presidents to red, white and blue stars cut from construction paper. Name the presidents and share a bit of information about each one. Send home a copy of the above prayer with the president stars.

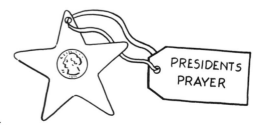

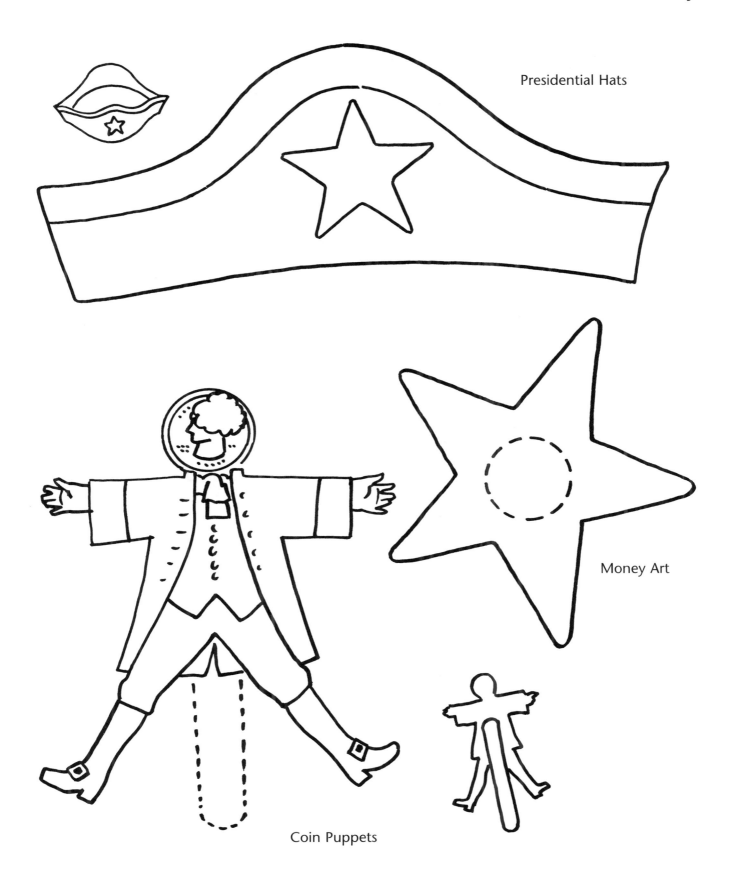

Presidential Hats

Money Art

Coin Puppets

Coin Puppets

Use the coins to make little puppets. Cut out the paper doll pattern provided below on heavy paper and glue the coins to the heads. Enhance the puppets with cotton for hair and beards and use felt and fabric scraps to make clothing.

February 18 – Blessed Fra Angelico

This holy man was named Guido de Piero as a child, but when he became a Dominican monk, his name was changed to Fra Giovanni (Brother John). But that name didn't stick either, for the other monks always called him "Fra Angelico." This was because they thought he was holy like the angels, and that his paintings were so beautiful it was as if angels painted them. In fact, that great artist, Michelangelo, said that Fra Angelico must have gone to heaven to find the people who were the models for his paintings!

Fra Angelico painted scenes from the Bible and of saints' lives for a monastery and many other places. He used vivid colors, including gold, and the portraits he painted were life-like, but it was not for beauty that he painted. He hoped that his paintings would help people love God and pray more. It is said that when he finished a painting, he would never go back to change it, because he felt God directed him in painting it in the first place. Changing it would not be what God wanted.

Activity: Angelico Inspirations

Bring in some art books that contain paintings by Fra Angelico, or if possible, hang a print in the classroom. Then offer children paints and paper. Together, say a prayer, thanking God for the ability to make pictures. Then encourage the children to paint. You could encourage the older children to choose a biblical or saint story to paint. Hang the finished paintings with the art print.

March

March at a Glance
Dedication of the Month: St. Joseph
March's Liturgical Colors
Patron Saints of the Month
March 4: St. Casimir
March 17: St. Patrick
March 19: St. Joseph and Celebration Table Ideas
March 20: First Day of Spring
March 20/21: The Vernal Equinox
March 24: Archbishop Oscar Romero,
March 25: Annunciation of the Lord
March 30: Sister Thea Bowman

Dedication for March: St. Joseph
St. Joseph is well loved for being an understanding and supportive husband to Mary and protector and teacher to young Jesus. In addition to his feast day in March, Joseph is recognized and celebrated on the Feast of the Holy Family during the week of Christmas, as well as on May 1st, the feast of St. Joseph the Worker.

March's Liturgical Colors
Ordinary Time: Green
Green is the color of hope and life.
Lent: Purple
Purple is used during Lent to symbolize penance and sacrifice.

Patron Saints of the Month
March 4: Casimir: unmarried men, kings and princes, Lithuania
March 8: John of God: booksellers, heart patients, hospital workers, printers, sick people
March 9: Frances of Rome: motorists
March 17: Patrick: Ireland
March 19: Joseph: charity to the poor, a happy home, peace, carpenters, workers, Belgium, Canada, China, Peru

March 4 – St. Casimir

St. Casimir was a prince in Poland in the 1400's. His teacher could see that Casimir would become a great leader and that he wanted to nurture Casimir's ability to make good decisions. So the teacher taught Casimir to understand and follow God's laws. The prince chose not to live with riches, and he prayed for hours each day. By the time he was 13, even people in other countries knew that Casimir would be a good king. At this young age, he came to believe that war was wrong. He became what is called a "conscientious objector," and he refused to take part in any war. In his short life, he was a fair and peaceful ruler, who especially loved Our Lady. He died of an illness when he was only 23.

Here is a story about how Casimir made a brave decision about war.

Story: The Prince Turns Back

Prince Casimir stood before his father, the King of Poland.

"I have received word that there are many in our neighboring country of Hungary who are unhappy with their king. These people have heard of you—that you are a young man of wisdom and goodness. They want you to become their king!"

"But I am only 13 years old!" Casimir exclaimed.

His father nodded proudly. "A wise thirteen-year-old!" he said. "Besides, you will gain treasure for our family and great honor, too. I am getting an army ready for you to take to the border of Hungary. You are to take over Hungary and become king."

Casimir knew all about the fighting that went on between countries then and did as he was told. However, it did not take him long to see great problems. His soldiers were paid very little. Frustrated, some ran away. Now that he was near Hungary, he learned that the current king was putting together a large army to fight Casimir.

"My army is small and getting smaller. If we fight this other army, my soldiers don't have much chance of winning—only of dying," Casimir reasoned. "And why will they die? Doesn't the king of Hungary have a right to stay on the throne? I cannot believe the right thing here is to fight, and lose all these men."

With that, he turned his army around and marched back home.

His father was furious and embarrassed. He punished his son by sending him away to another castle for three months. There, Casimir continued to pray and study. He decided then he would never again be involved in war.

Discussion Starter: What did St. Casimir think was the right thing to do when it came to fighting?

March 17 – St. Patrick

St. Patrick, a patron saint of Ireland, was born in Britain. When he was 16, he was forced to go to Ireland to be a slave there. For six years, he took care of sheep and was very lonely. He prayed often and felt God's strong love. Eventually he escaped and went back to Britain. Then he decided to study to become a priest and teacher, so he could go back to Ireland to teach others there about Jesus. And Patrick became such an incredible teacher that because of him, almost all the people in Ireland became Christian!

Activity: *Breastplate of St. Patrick*

There is a prayer called the "Breastplate of St. Patrick." Part of it is particularly good for helping children feel Jesus' closeness. Make booklets using the words below, copying one for each child. Read the prayer to the children, and then have them illustrate themselves with Jesus according to the words. Talk about how they can draw some of the more symbolic verses.

Words for the booklet:

Cover: Prayer of St. Patrick

Page 1: Christ be with me
   Christ within me

Page 2: Christ behind me
   Christ before me
   Christ beside me

Page 3: Christ to win me
   Christ to comfort me

Page 4: Christ beneath me
   Christ above me

Page 5: Christ with me in quiet times

Page 6: Christ with me in dangerous times

Page 7: Christ in the hearts of all who love me

March 19 – St. Joseph

Long ago, in Bible times, the most wonderful compliment that could be given was to call someone a "tzaddik," which was a person of justice and virtue. In the Gospel of St. Matthew, St. Joseph is called a just man. Perhaps that is why he was chosen for the big, all-important job of being Jesus' earthly father. He protected Jesus and Mary when they had to travel when Jesus was still a baby. He worked hard as a carpenter so the family had food, clothing and a place to live. And, he taught Jesus how to be a carpenter. St. Joseph did a wonderful job of taking care of Mary and Jesus, and because of this he is loved and celebrated. Many people ask St. Joseph to pray for them.

There are stories and traditions around St. Joseph. Here is a famous story, taken from the Gospel of James, a Christian writing written about the year 170, which is not part of the Scriptures.

Legend: St. Joseph's Lilies

Mary, the daughter of Anne and Joachim, was now old enough to get married. In those days, parents or a priest chose the person a girl was to marry. The high priest Zacharias was to decide on Mary's husband. He knew that God had brought Mary into the world for a special reason, so he prayed, asking God to help him make the right choice for Mary.

An angel came to him and said, "Call all the men that you can choose from to come to the temple. Tell each one to bring his walking stick. God will use the sticks to give you a sign of which man should be the husband of Mary."

So all the men arrived with their walking sticks, and left them there as Zacharias requested. Among them was a good person named Joseph, who was a carpenter.

In the morning, all the walking sticks were still lined up, except for one, from which beautiful lilies had blossomed during the night! This stick belonged to Joseph. Zacharias the high priest knew then that Joseph was the man God had chosen for Mary.

Traditions

When some people from Sicily came to live in the United States, they brought with them a wonderful tradition of offering hospitality on the feast day of St. Joseph. In a home, the family table is extended to its greatest length and moved against a wall. A statue of St. Joseph is placed there, surrounded by candles and flowers. Much food is prepared and many guests come to eat. They move on, leaving room for others to come and eat. If the guests leave any gifts of money, this money is given to those who are needy.

Birds called swallows have their own St. Joseph Day tradition. In California, there is a church called Mission San Juan Capistrano. Every year on March 19, on the feast of St. Joseph, the swallows fly in after a winter away. There they build their nests in the church's eaves. On October 23 they head south for the winter.

Every year from March 15 to 20, a village in Honduras, Copan Ruinas, holds a fair in honor of its patron saint, San Jose, or St. Joseph. The celebration mixes traditions from the peoples' Mayan and Spanish heritages. There is much food, piñatas, dancing and music. On March 19, the village people gather for an outdoor Mass. Then, a statue of San Jose is carried through the crowded streets, dressed in a straw hat and black cape. Consider having a small procession in the classroom or at home by having children take turns carrying a St. Joseph statue.

The Celebration Table

Place a statue of St. Joseph on your Celebration Table, add candles and flowers, like the Sicilian table of hospitality. Help children think of symbols of St. Joseph that could be added (e.g., small pieces of wood and a hammer, or even a drawing of swallows).

March 20 – First Day of Spring

"For low the winter is past, the rain is over and gone.
The flowers appear on the earth, the time of singing has come,
and the voice of the turtledove is heard in our land." Song of Songs 2:11,12

The season of spring begins March 20 and ends June 21. During the spring we experience the days getting longer and warmer. In most areas of the country we see the grass becoming green, buds coming out on the trees and flowers beginning to sprout. Various birds and ducks and geese are returning to their summer homes.

Prayer

Spring is in the air! The days are getting longer and warmer and we are beginning to see bits of new life in the grass and trees. Thank you, God, for springtime! We pray that our hearts will be filled with hope and joy as this new season begins. Amen.

Activities
Springtime Discussion
Talk about all of the new life we see in spring. What changes do we see? What do we get to do in spring that we can't do at other times of the year?

Nature Walk
Take a nature walk and look for signs of spring. Watch for buds on the trees, birds that have returned from winter destinations, green plants and grass that are just beginning to grow.

"April Showers"
Plan your spring themes around the saying, "April showers bring May flowers." Cover a large golf umbrella with crepe paper or tissue paper. Gather the paper around the top of the umbrella and hold in place with a bow. Fasten the sides down with tape. Using the pattern provided, have the children cut out raindrop shapes from different shades of blue paper. On each raindrop write a sign of spring or new life. Write each child's name on a raindrop, too. Hang the raindrops with clear fishing line around the outside and in the inside of the umbrella. Hang the decorated umbrella from the ceiling over your prayer corner or tape it to the back of a high back chair. Write, "Thank You, God, for Spring" on a strip of paper to fasten to the top of the umbrella. Continue the theme with bulletin boards, etc. Cut out large raindrops from white construction paper. Have the children paint them with watercolor designs and hang around the room.

Planting Season
Plant grass seed in paper cups or small clay flowerpots. Watch the grass grow tall and have the children "mow" or cut it with a scissors if it gets too long. Have each child cut out a colored flower and glue a photo of him or herself to the center of the flower. Staple or tape the flower to a straw or dowel and place it in the center of the pot of grass. If the grass is growing well by Easter, place a plastic egg containing a treat and/or an Easter blessing on it and send it home.

Don't forget to plant any seeds you may have collected in the fall from dried flowers. Review the cycle of life using the flower as an example. The flower must die in order to make new seeds to grow new flowers.

Flower Garden

Make a terraced flower garden for your classroom. Purchase three clay flowerpots in graduated sizes. Begin with the smallest being about 8 inches and the other three being 12 inch, 16 inch or 18 inch widths. Prepare each pot for planting. Place a few pebbles in the bottom of the pot and then fill with potting soil to within two inches of the top. Put the largest pot in a saucer and place the next largest on top of that and the next largest on top of that. Plant bedding plants or seeds in the top pot and around the edges of the other two. You might want to place a vine in one of the top two levels. Give each child a flower to help plant and mark it with the child's name on a craft stick. Place your plant tower in a sunny spot inside or out and take turns watering. Place a "Welcome to Spring," sign on the top of the planter.

Plant Markers

To bring color to the garden while waiting for the seeds to grow, make plant markers with the children. Use craft foam or heavy colored paper to cut out different flower shapes. Write each child's name on the center of her or his flower cutout. If you have used paper, cover the cutout with clear contact paper. Tape or staple the flower to the top of a dowel, paint stick or large craft stick and mark each child's plant in the planter or garden.

March 20/21 – The Vernal Equinox

We have once again arrived at one of the two days in the entire year when day and night are each exactly 12 hours long. The word "equinox" comes from the word "equal" as the day and night are equal in time. From now until the autumn equinox, the nights get shorter and days get longer. This equinox usually occurs in Lent, the word "Lent" having come from the word "lengthen." The word "Lent" is also a very old word for springtime.

March 24 – Archbishop Oscar Romero

Oscar Romero had a challenging job: he became archbishop of San Salvador, in the country of El Salvador. Oscar was a quiet, prayerful man, but his country was filled with violence. The small number of very rich people ruled the large number of very poor people. This lop-

sided government used fear and force to keep going. No one expected the shy new archbishop to try to change this. But soon after Oscar became archbishop, a friend of his was killed because he was working for fairness for poor people. This touched Oscar deeply. He began speaking at churches and on the radio about these problems. People who were in power began to hate him. Other people loved him.

The archbishop knew all about the danger in his country, and he knew that because of his talks, he too was in danger. With some fear and much courage, he chose to keep speaking out, for he believed strongly that that is what Jesus would do. And, as Jesus died, so was Archbishop Romero killed in 1980 for the work he did. He is remembered and greatly loved today by many people in El Salvador. March 24 is the anniversary of his death.

Discussion Starter: Whom did Archbishop Romero look to for guidance?

March 25 – Annunciation of the Lord

In the sixth month, the angel Gabriel was sent from God to a city of Galilee named Nazareth, to a virgin betrothed to a man whose name was Joseph, of the house of David; and the virgin's name was Mary. And he came to her and said, "Hail, O favored one, the Lord is with you!" But she was greatly troubled at the saying, and considered in her mind what sort of greeting this might be. And the angel said to her, "Do not be afraid, Mary, for you have found favor with God. And behold, you will conceive in your womb and bear a son and you shall call his name Jesus. He will be great, and will be called the Son of the Most High; and the Lord God will give to him the throne of his father David, and he will reign over the house of Jacob for ever; and of his kingdom there will be no end." Luke 1:26-33

The Annunciation of the Lord is the day we celebrate the announcement to Mary that she had been chosen to be the Mother of Jesus. The angel Gabriel visited Mary and told her that the baby would be conceived by the Holy Spirit. The angel also told Mary that the baby's name would be Jesus and he would be the savior of the world.

Prayer

Just think how scared Mary must have been when the angel Gabriel visited her and told her she was going to have a baby. How she must have loved God to say yes to the request to be the mother of Jesus. Holy Mary, Mother of God, we ask you to pray for us today. We ask that as we learn more about Jesus, we too will be able to say yes to God as you did. We ask this prayer in your name, sweet Mary. Amen.

Activities
Annunciation Celebration

Celebrate the Annunciation with spring in mind. Mary found out she was to bring forth new life during the time of year we look for new life, in the spring time. Try planting seeds that will tolerate the cold days and nights of spring. Plant pansies in pots that can be brought in and out depending on the weather. Cut pussy willow or lilac branches for your prayer corner. These are early bloomers and fun to watch.

Mini-pilgrimage

Pray the above prayer or a Hail Mary at an altar or statue you may have in your church that is dedicated to Mary. Leave flowers there or special petitions your class may have.

Marian Bulletin Board

Make a special bulletin board of Mary pictures. Have the children go through old Christmas cards to find pictures of Mary. Fasten these to a bulletin board or poster board and title it "Holy Mary, the Lord is with you."

Prayer Pots

Make copies of the Hail Mary prayer on 3" by 5" card stock. Tie these to small votive candles for home as a reminder of the day. Place the candles in small clay flowerpots decorated with glitter paint. On the top rim of the pot write "Holy Mary, pray for us," with marker.

March 30 – Sister Thea Bowman

Bertha Bowman was baptized Catholic when she was ten years old. Later, she made a decision to become a sister, which surprised her family and friends. After all, she would be the only African-American nun in the whole convent. All the other sisters were white, or European-American. How would she fit in? Bertha, or Sister Thea (she took this name when she became a sister, and it means "of God") had her own way of fitting in. She was just herself, knowing that everything about her was a gift from God. She knew that being Catholic and African-American was a great gift she brought to the Church.

Sister Thea became an excellent speaker, singer, and storyteller. She spoke to hundreds of people who loved her, listened to her and sang with her. They came to see how important African-Americans are to the Catholic Church.

This is the anniversary of her death.

Discussion Starter: What were some of the things that Sister Thea did well?

Lent at a Glance

Mardi Gras / Fat Tuesday / Shrove Tuesday / Pancake Day

All refer to the day before Ash Wednesday, the first day of Lent.

Mardi Gras is French for Fat Tuesday. While Fat Tuesday is the day before Ash Wednesday, Mardi Gras in some places reflects at least two weeks of carnival before the serious more disciplined days of Lent. New Orleans is known for its very festive Mardi Gras, which includes parades, dances and lots of celebrating.

Shrove Tuesday refers to the Shriving Bell, which rang to bring everyone to church to be shriven, or to confess his or her sins before the season of Lent. Early Christians observed strict rules of fasting and self-denial during Lent, so in the days before, they would eat restricted foods, party and have fun.

In England people used up the rich foods of eggs, butter and milk (from which they fasted during Lent) to make pancakes. In some American and English towns folks still celebrate by eating pancakes and running a Pancake Race. People line up at the start of the race with a large pancake in a fry pan. While running the racer must flip the pancake three times in the air before the finish.

Prayer

On this day of Mardi Gras, we celebrate with family and friends. What a blessing it is to have fun with some of the special people in our lives. As we look ahead to Lent, our preparation for Easter, we ask Jesus to be in our hearts as we grow to be closer to him. Amen.

Lent

A Story for Fat Tuesday That Will Carry You Into Ash Wednesday

Use the patterns provided to help you tell the story. Copy, enlarge and cut out each pattern. Allow the children to focus on each pattern as it is mentioned in the story.

Story: A Time for Silliness, A Time for Stillness

"Today is Mardi Gras!" sang Danny at breakfast.

"No, it's not, it's Carnival!" argued his sister Jenna.

As their father buttered toast, he said, "You are both right. Mardi Gras and Carnival are the same celebration."

"We get to be silly tonight," Jenna said.

"And eat lots and lots of pancakes!" Danny added.

"You are both right again," said Daddy. "Tomorrow we start Lent, a time when we think seriously about Jesus' life and how we can make our own lives more like Jesus'. Long ago, people did not eat meat, eggs or butter during Lent, so they ate up all that they had the day before and had a party to say good-bye to the meat."

"Bye-bye, meat!" Danny sang.

"What does Mardi Gras mean?" Jenna asked.

"'Mardi' is Tuesday in French, and 'Gras' means fat—Fat Tuesday, the day before Lent when you eat up all the foods with fat."

"Fat Tuesday!" Jenna shouted. Both children burst into giggles.

Later that day, Danny and Jenna came into the kitchen. Daddy was flipping pancakes. On the table sat blueberry syrup, ice cream, maple syrup, butter, peanuts and whipped cream. Daddy put a large stack of pancakes and a plate of sausages on the table. And then, they feasted until the

pancakes were gone, their fingers were sticky, and their tummies full.

"Time for the silliness?" Jenna asked.

Daddy brought out markers, glitter, and feathers. He cut out cardboard masks and they decorated them. When the masks were ready to wear, they put on loud, fast music and danced and danced, sang songs, and banged pots and pans together and sang some more.

When they collapsed on the couch, giggling, Daddy said Carnival was over. He turned off the music and took off the masks. "Go wash your hands and faces and come back in here," he said.

When Jenna and Danny returned, they found the living room quiet and darkened except for one candle. Daddy was sitting near it, and they sat down by him.

"Carnival is over, Lent is beginning. We ask Jesus to help us have a holy Lent so we will be ready for the joy of Easter," Daddy said. "Now, we will go to bed quietly. No story tonight, no songs, just this holy, special stillness."

He kissed Danny and then Jenna, and silently they went up to bed.

Activities
Carnival

Plan a carnival in your classroom. Invite the children to bring in masks and/or costumes to wear. Decorate your room with balloons and crepe paper to make it look festive. Plan a few party games and serve a special snack.

Pancakes

Make pancakes for snack and serve a couple of different toppings such as strawberries and syrups.

Races

Plan a race using a wet (not dripping) sponge cut into a pancake shape and kid size pan. Have the children toss the pancake (from the pan) two or three times in the air as they run across the room.

Masks

Make masks to wear for the day. Purchase plain party masks and have the children decorate them with stickers, feathers and glitter. To make your own masks, cut a large paper plate in half and cut out two holes for eyes in the center of the half plate. Glue a craft stick to the bottom of one side of the plate. The children will hold the stick to put the mask to their face. Decorate the mask with markers, beads or glitter.

Take It Home

Send home a copy of the Mardi Gras prayer from page 115, attached to a party horn or hat.

Liturgical Color

Purple is used during Lent for the vestments and various parts of the Church to symbolize penance and sacrifice.

Ash Wednesday

"Yet even now, says the Lord, return to me with your whole heart." (Joel 2:12)

Historically called the Day of Ashes, Ash Wednesday marks the beginning of Lent. There are 7 Wednesdays and 40 days (excluding Sundays) before Easter. The significance of the forty days comes from Jesus spending 40 days in the wilderness before beginning his public ministry.

On this day early Christians declared their sinfulness and desire for forgiveness to their community. They wore sackcloth and covered themselves with ashes as symbols of their unworthiness.

Today we observe Ash Wednesday by having the mark of the cross made on our forehead with ashes. Palm branches from the previous Palm Sunday are burned to make the ashes. The ashes are a symbol of sadness and death. The cross reminds us that we belong to Jesus who died for all humankind on the cross.

Prayer

Ash Wednesday is a day to remember how much Jesus loved us and the sacrifice he made for us. Today also marks the beginning of Lent, a time when we prepare for Easter. As the Sign of the Cross is marked on our foreheads, we pray that we will turn away from sin and grow closer to Jesus during this special season. Amen.

Lent: "to lengthen"

Around A.D. 400, the Christian church formally established the season of Lent. It begins Ash Wednesday, which is 40 days (not including Sundays) before Easter. The word "Lent" means lengthen and it is also an old English word for spring. In spring the days get longer, brighter and warmer, and we experience new life everywhere in nature. What a great connection to the new life we as Christians have in Jesus.

Early Christians were very penitent during Lent. People were somber, strictly fasted for the whole 40 days and even wore sackcloth, a rough fabric similar to burlap. Today we are more relaxed with the fasting and have a less solemn attitude. During Lent we try to become better people and grow closer to Jesus by giving up negative attributes or taking on positive ones.

Activities
Lenten Discussion

Discuss Ash Wednesday and Lent. Talk about how we can grow closer to God. Explain that during this time we give up and take on habits that will help us be better people. Ask the children to think about one thing they can do to grow closer to Jesus during Lent. Write these down and refer to them in prayer as the weeks go by.

Ashes

Prepare a bowl of ashes and make the Sign of the Cross on the foreheads of the children. Give the children a sticker of a cross to wear on their shirts or shoes as a reminder of Ash Wednesday.

Burlap Crosses

Purchase burlap from a fabric store. Tell the children that early Christians wore clothes made out of a similar material during Lent. The rough cloth reminded people to think of Jesus. Trace and cut crosses about 3" by 5." Attach a safety pin and have the kids wear the cross as a Lenten reminder.

Lenten Signs

On yellow paper make a Lenten road sign that says, "Turn to Jesus." Use the pattern provided to make a large turn arrow. Hang these around your building or send them home as a Lenten reminder.
"Turn to Jesus" or "Turn to Jesus in Prayer." Lent 20__.

Lenten Candles

Make a focal point for your prayer corner by placing seven thick candles in a box or cake pan of sand. Light one candle a week during Lent and light the seventh candle Easter week. Add small silk or real flowers to the sand to celebrate new life during the Easter season.

Nature Walk

Take a nature walk and talk about the changes that go on in nature when spring arrives. Notice the buds on the trees, green grass, flowers starting to sprout and birds returning from the south. Take grocery bags and pick up the trash that appears once the snow melts.

Service Project

Plan a service project collection for the Lenten season. Encourage the children to bring in personal hygiene items for your local shelter or food pantry. Toothbrushes, toothpaste, combs, bubble bath, etc. are always needed items. A sock, Teddy Bear or play ball collection would also be meaningful to the children. Collect these items near your prayer corner so everyone can see the success of your project.

Change of Pace

Pray these weekly Lenten prayers in a place other than your classroom. Sit on the altar steps or other area of the church you don't normally go such as the balcony or side altar.

Celebration Table Ideas

Use a simple purple cloth to cover the table. On this, place a small cross (you can easily make one from small sticks and thread), a cactus plant (warn children of the painful results of touching a cactus), and a candle. At group time, light the candle. Read Scripture stories that show Jesus' love and compassion for the poor, the handicapped, the young.

Lenten Resolutions

It is a Catholic custom to make resolutions involving penance or acts of kindness or charity during the season of Lent. Some Catholics choose to give something up such as candy. Others try to correct a bad habit such as talking negatively about others. Still others take on a helpful task such as volunteering to help with the local food pantry.

Activity: *Lenten Action!*

Inspire the children into Lenten action by decorating your room with acts of Lenten kindness. Make a garland of paper hands— one hand for each child. Hang the garland along a wall high enough to be out of reach.

Ask the children to offer ideas for Lenten resolutions. This would include an act of love or service or sacrificing something. Examples might be to visit someone elderly on a regular basis, volunteer in the church nursery, shovel someone's walk, pray more often each day or give up pop, a favorite TV show or candy. Give each child a hand from the garland. Invite the children to open the hands and write their Lenten resolutions in the middle of a heart that you have drawn on the inside of the hand. Then hang the hands back on the garland as a reminder of their Lenten resolutions.

Simple Meal and Plays

The following activities can be easily modified to use at home, with one family or with a gathering of families.

Lent is a good time to talk with children about sharing. It is also a good time to gather for a simple meal and prayer. Invite the families of your program to a soup supper. You provide the soup and ask your guests to bring loaves of bread to share. Encourage families also to contribute the money that they would have spent on a more elaborate meal. Have an offering basket, explaining that the money collected will be sent to a program that helps alleviate hunger. Make sure the children understand that they are sharing their meal money. Before eating, put on the following plays which focus on sharing. Only the narrator speaks, and the acting parts are designed so young children can easily participate. A few quick rehearsals with children before the dinner would suffice.

Play #1

This play is based on the Gospel story of Jesus feeding thousands of people with a miracle. You will need one adult to play Jesus. Have him seated on a chair. Choose two children to stand behind him as apostles. The rest of the children can be members of the crowd, and should sit on the floor in front of Jesus. Have a basket near the apostles, which contains a loaf of bread that has not been sliced. Another adult should be the narrator.

The Miracle of the Loaves and Fishes
(Note: The narrator's words are not in bold.)

All day, large numbers of people were coming to Jesus. He healed many sick people. **HAVE THREE CHILDREN COME FORWARD TO JESUS, WHO LAYS HIS HANDS ON THEM. THEY THEN SIT BACK DOWN**. Now it was getting late. One of Jesus' apostles said to him, "Lord, maybe you should tell all the people to leave so they can go and buy something to eat."

Jesus said to his apostles, "There is no need of that. Give them some food yourselves."

"There are only five loaves of bread and two fish!" said an apostle.

"Bring them to me," Jesus answered. **ONE APOSTLE GIVES JESUS THE BASKET WITH THE LOAF OF BREAD**. Jesus took the food, looked up to heaven and said a blessing. **JESUS BREAKS THE LOAF OF BREAD FOR ALL TO SEE**. He broke the loaves of bread and gave them to the apostles who began giving the food to the crowd. **THE APOSTLES SHOULD WALK AMONGST THE CROWD WITH THE TWO HALVES OF BREAD, BREAKING OFF SMALL PIECES AND GIVING THEM TO THE CHILDREN**. There was enough for the thousands of people, and there was even food left over!

Play #2
This play is based on a story of a holy man named St. Isadore who lived in Spain in the twelfth century. Before starting, the narrator should encourage the audience to join in on Isadore's repeated line. Choose one child to be Isadore, then line up other children into five groups of three, Groups A through E. Four of these groups will join Isadore on his walk to church, so they should be stationed at separate points from where Isadore begins and where he stops. The end point will be a simple scene at a church dinner. The remaining group will be at the church dinner, standing behind a small table. This table stands on the opposite side of the room from where Isadore begins. Place some pots, pans, and dishes on the table as props for Isadore's church dinner.

Dinner for Isadore
NARRATOR: Long ago in Spain, there lived a good man named Isadore. He loved Jesus very much. Each day, he prayed in the morning before work. Then he went off to plow fields for a rich man and he prayed while he plowed. Isadore himself was poor. Still, as soon as he saw someone poorer than he, Isadore gave them his food or some clothing. Here is a story about him.

CHILD WHO PLAYS ISADORE BEGINS TO WALK TOWARDS GROUP A. One day, Isadore was walking to his church. He was looking forward to the dinner they were giving there. Soon he met a woman and her two children. They were hungry. **GROUP A JOINS ISADORE.**

"Come along with me to the church. There will be plenty of food there!" said Isadore. So they came along.

THEY ALL MOVE ONTO GROUP B. Soon they met three men. They were hungry too. **GROUP B JOINS ISADORE AND THE OTHERS.**

NARRATOR AND AUDIENCE: "Come along with us to the church. There will be plenty of food there!" they said. **THEY ALL MOVE ONTO GROUP C.**

NARRATOR: Soon they met three teenagers. They were hungry also. **GROUP C JOINS THE OTHERS.**

NARRATOR AND AUDIENCE: "Come along with us to the church. There will be plenty of food there!" they said. **THEY MOVE ONTO GROUP D.**

NARRATOR: Soon they met three women who were hungry. **GROUP D JOINS THE OTHERS.**

NARRATOR AND AUDIENCE: "Come along with us to the church. There will be plenty of food there!" they said.

NARRATOR: Isadore and his new friends arrived at the church. **ALL WALK OVER TO THE TABLE WHERE GROUP E WAITS.** "We are hungry!" Isadore said cheerfully.

"Isadore!" exclaimed the church people. "Who are all these people? There will never be enough food for us and them too!"

"God will provide," Isadore replied.

And God did. There was enough food for everyone! And Isadore smiled.

Palm Sunday
Sunday before Easter

"Hosanna to the Son of David!
Blessed is he who comes in the name of the Lord!
Hosanna in the highest!" Matthew 21:9

Early Christians celebrated Holy Week by retracing the events of Jesus' final days before Easter. By the 300s Palm Sunday processions through Jerusalem were held on the Sunday before Easter.

In modern times Christians observe Palm Sunday by handing out palm branches and processing in their churches. Red, the color for royalty, is worn on vestments, etc.

On Palm Sunday we celebrate the triumphant entrance of Jesus into Jerusalem the week before Easter. People praised him with the word "Hosanna" and proclaimed him their new king. As was the tradition for royalty and heroes, palm branches and clothing were laid on the road for him to walk on. It is hard to believe that those same people crucified him five days later.

Prayer

Dear Jesus, today we remember your humble but triumphant entrance into Jerusalem. You truly are the Son of God, the Messiah. We will keep you in our hearts this week as we remember your Holy Week journey so many years ago. Hosanna! Hosanna! to Jesus our King! Amen.

Activities
Palm Sunday Procession

Plan a Palm Sunday procession through your building or around the block. Have the children carry palm branches and a sign that says "Hosanna! Glory to the King!" If your classes meet on Sunday morning arrange to have the children in your program process through church with palms during the opening hymn.

Palm Sunday Banner

Make a Palm Sunday banner by having the children make green hand prints (for palm branches) on a banner titled, "Blessed Is He Who Comes In The Name of the Lord, Hosanna!" Hang the banner in a central location for all to see.

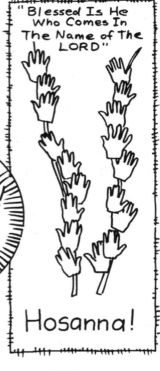

Take-Home Banners

To make a banner for home, have the children put their green handprint on the middle of a paper plate. After the paint has dried write the word, "Hosanna." Punch a hole at the top of the plate and lace a piece of yarn through it for hanging.

Basket Collection

Invite families to bring in food for the food pantry in their Easter baskets. Collect the food and give the children and their empty baskets a blessing for the week ahead. Send a little Easter prayer and treat home with each basket.

Basket Blessing

Dear Lord, bless these children and the food and baskets they have brought today. We thank you for the opportunity to share with others. In celebration of Easter, these baskets will be full of eggs and other goodies. Help us to keep Jesus in our hearts as we enjoy our baskets and celebrate the new life we have in him. Amen.

Holy Week

The week leading to Easter is the richest time of the year for Christians. Filled with symbols of triumph, tragedy, fear, and incredible love, it can be an emotional and spiritual time for adults. For young children, the full magnitude of this time cannot be realized yet, but we can begin to introduce them to the Scripture stories and symbols that best portray what Christianity is all about.

Offer children a "path of Holy Week" in your home or classroom. Set up stopping points, or stations, which represent the different events of the week. The stations are similar in idea to the Celebration Table. Start with a Palm Sunday station, and each day add another (Holy Thursday, Good Friday, Easter vigil.) That way you can focus well on each by introducing the new one each day, yet the children can return to the others if they have need to. Here are stories to read with children for each station and suggestions for appropriate ways to set up each station. Introduce the station by gathering the children around it and reading the story. Emphasize that these stations are quiet places. They are welcome to return if they sit quietly and touch the symbols gently.

Palm Sunday Station
The Story

On Palm Sunday, we remember when Jesus arrived in the city of Jerusalem. Many people loved Jesus. They knew that he was extra special! When he came to the city, they were very excited. He rode in on a donkey, and many went to greet him. They shouted, "Hosanna! Hosanna! as they praised God for all the wonderful things Jesus had done. They waved branches taken from trees to show honor to Jesus, and a large crowd followed him into Jerusalem.

The Station

Cover a small table or sturdy box with a green cloth. Set the table with a figure of a donkey or colt (check your nativity set) and a strip of paper on which the word "Hosanna" is written in colorful block letters. Include palm branches, if available. If not, use a lush growing plant.

Holy Thursday Station
The Story

On Holy Thursday, we remember the special dinner Jesus had with his friends. Jesus knew that he would soon die. He wanted to show his friends how much he loved them. Jesus also wanted to teach them how they were to treat other people. So, at dinner, he took a bowl of water and a towel and he washed their feet! They understood Jesus was asking them to love and help others. Then Jesus broke his bread and shared it with them.

The Station

On a purple cloth, place a piece of flat bread on a plate ("pocket bread" is a good choice), a bowl of water and a towel.

Good Friday Station
The Story

On Good Friday, we remember the day that Jesus died. His friends were very sad. They lovingly buried his body in a tomb.

The Station

on a black cloth, place a simple cross, perhaps laying it across some small stones.

Holy Saturday Station
The Story

On Holy Saturday, we wait for Easter, the day we celebrate Jesus' rising from the dead. That will be a joyful day, but Holy Saturday is a quiet, thoughtful day. We think of Jesus' friends who did not know that he would rise from the dead. They were very sad. We think about how Jesus loves us so very, very much.

The Station

Fashion a tomb with building blocks. Place the tomb on a plain white cloth, with a stone "rolled" in front of the door. Add a small bouquet of flowers.

A tomb can also be made with papier-mâché: invert a mixing bowl and cover the rounded part with aluminum foil; apply two or three layers of papier-mâché over the foil; when it is dry, remove the bowl, and cut a small door into the papier-mâché frame; paint the frame with acrylic paints, using gray and brown to simulate stone.

Good Friday

From noon on, darkness fell over the land and Jesus gave up his spirit and died.
Matthew 27: 45,50

Good Friday may have originally been called God's Friday, as the English word for good comes from the word God. Christians around the world observe Good Friday, the solemn day of Christ's crucifixion.

Over the centuries and throughout the world, there have been many ways Good Friday has been observed. In the Netherlands, people planted snow peas on Good Friday as a sign of the new life that comes to us through Jesus' death and resurrection. Good Friday is sometimes called Marble Day in England. The traditional story goes that priests gave children in their town marbles so that they would play quietly on Good Friday afternoon. Marbles were even available in the pubs to keep the adults quiet. In more modern times businesses were closed between the hours of 12pm and 3pm, symbolic of the remembrance of Jesus' death.

Prayer

On this holy and solemn day, we remember that Jesus died for us. We recall the "Good" that came to all people when Jesus died. We pray that we will always turn to Jesus and follow in His footsteps to happiness. In the name of Jesus we pray. Amen.

Activities
Making Crosses

Tie sticks together with raffia or leather thongs to make a cross. Attach the above prayer and send home.

Reverence for Jesus

Make a conscious effort to play quiet games on Good Friday afternoon as a sign of reverence for Jesus. Tell the children the marble story and play marbles with them. Provide puzzles or other board games that would offer quiet activities for the afternoon.

Indoor Plant

Grow an indoor sweet potato plant. Put three or four sturdy toothpicks around the middle of a sweet potato. Fill a canning jar with water and place the potato in the jar. The toothpicks will hold half of the potato out of the water. Place in the sunlight and keep the jar full of water. In a few days leaves will sprout from the top of the potato.

Holy Saturday
Preparing for the Resurrection

The story of Christ's crucifixion is confusing and frightening for preschoolers, who are particularly sensitive to death issues. However, as young Christians, it is imperative that they begin to experience the most profound truth of their faith: that Christ rose from the dead. As teachers and parents, we must pass on this story with reverence as well as skill.

The following suggestions are written for the classroom but could easily be adapted in the home. They are ways to prepare yourself, the environment, and the children for this story. The simple art activity is designed to allow children to express their understanding of the story they have just heard. Some may paint something directly related to the story; for others it may be symbolic, or simply a pleasurable activity as they ponder the story.

Prepare Yourself

Prepare yourself for this time by reading the Resurrection Scriptures (Mt 28-1-10; Mk 16:1-8; Lk 24:1-12 or Jn 20:1-18) by yourself. Because of the profound message of the resurrection, it can evoke strong emotions. As you read the Scriptures, look for the feelings of the biblical people and reflect on your own. You may experience grief, surprise, fear, wonder, awe and joy. Being aware of your own reactions helps you tell the story fully. Be prepared also, to lead children in singing a joy-filled "alleluia" when your story is finished.

Prepare Your Room

To involve children in the very emotion of this story, create a darkened space in which to sit: close shades, turn off lights, drape dark blankets on chairs outside the circle where the group will sit. In the center of this space, create a small "tomb." You can make one simply by covering a small basket or box with a dark towel, or be more elaborate with papier-mâché and paint on a cardboard box so it looks like stone, or build one of wood or wooden blocks. However you make it, have an entrance, and a real, large stone in front of it. Inside the tomb place a large, thick white candle. Keep matches with you (out of children's reach). The candle should not be visible to the children.

In another part of the room, set up paints, brushes, and paper for each child. Provide colors of great contrasts: white and yellow, black and brown as well as other colors.

Prepare the Children

If possible, do not let the children see the darkened space until it is time to tell the story. Then before bringing them in, explain that today you have a story that is so important they must come into a special place to hear it.

Lead them into the darkened space and encourage quiet listening. Sit in a circle surrounding the small tomb. Explain that today you will talk about the time when Jesus had died, and that where his body had been laid was a tomb made of stone. Have them look at the pretend tomb and think about what the real one was like. Explain also that a huge rock would have closed the entrance to the real tomb. That is how dead people were buried long ago in that part of the world.

Do not encourage any feelings that this dark space is scary, but rather that it is a prayerful, sacred place. Consider starting with a simple prayer, such as, "Dear Jesus, help us hear your special story. Amen." Use calming, deep-breathing exercises if little ones are restless. Then, tell the story.

Story: The Most Important Day

Jesus' friends were sad. Some were crying. Three days before, Jesus had died. Jesus had been their loving friend, the one who taught them about God and about living in a holy way. Now they missed him very much. What would they do without Jesus?

Mary Magdalene and Mary, James' mother, decided to go to the tomb where Jesus' body had been laid. The sun had barely begun to touch the sky, so they walked in the darkness and in sad silence.

They knew that a huge, heavy stone had been rolled in front of the tomb, a stone so massive they could never roll it away themselves. The two friends wondered how they could move it, for they wanted to visit Jesus' body once more. When they reached the tomb, there stood that great stone, cold, hard and unmoving.

Then the women felt a shaking of the earth under their feet.

Was it an earthquake? Frightened, they clung to each other.

"Look!" whispered Mary Magdalene. "The great stone has moved! And see? There is someone there!"

Both women stared, for now the stone lay on its side, the tomb stood open and on that stone sat an angel!

It is no small thing to see an angel. And this angel had a face that shone like lightening, and clothing that was as brilliant as snow in the sunshine!

The women still clung to each other, for they were very frightened. Yet they were also filled with wonder for here, where Jesus lay dead, was an angel sent by God!

"You don't need to be scared," the angel said. "You are looking for Jesus, but he is not here. He has risen."

Risen? But Jesus was dead! How could He rise? They were confused.

"Come and see where He lay," the angel invited. Holding onto each other, they came as close as they dared to the angel, and peeked into the dark, cold tomb. There was no body there, only the cloth that had covered it!

(At this point, stop talking and roll your stone away from the little tomb. Have children look inside. Then, lift the tomb up, revealing the candle. Set the tomb aside and light the candle, leaving it lit for the rest of the story.)

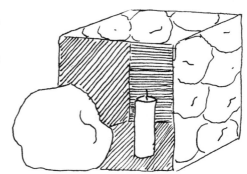

Jesus had risen! He had done what no human had ever done! He had been dead, and now He was alive!

They turned from the darkness of the tomb to the dazzling light of the angel. They were filled with joy and wonder as strong as the angel's light.

"Go now," said the angel. "And tell Peter and the other friends that Jesus has risen from the dead!"

(Now begin to sing "Alleluia!" Sing it several times. Then carrying the candle, lead the children to the art station and encourage them to paint.)

The Resurrection Party

The Church celebrates Easter for fifty days, so after your children return to your classroom following Easter, it is still very appropriate to observe it then. Once you have given the children a visual and verbal understanding of the days preceding Easter, it is important to follow through with a similar, yet more celebrative, experience of Easter.

Story: Jesus Rose!

Early in the morning, the third day after Jesus died, three of Jesus' friends went to his tomb. Yesterday the tomb had a great big, heavy rock in front if it, but this morning, it was laying on the ground! The friends hurried into the tomb. Jesus' body was gone! Two dazzling angels appeared. "Jesus is not here," the angels told them. "He is risen. Before he died, he said he would rise again, on the third day." The friends were amazed. No one had ever done this before! They understood now that Jesus was very, very special! Jesus was truly God!

Setting

Once again, use a small table, putting it in a place of honor. Cover it with a beautiful white cloth. Place the tomb on this, rolling the stone away from the door (you can do this as you tell the story). Add a figure or picture of the Risen Christ. Have plenty of fresh flowers behind the tomb and the picture.

Create a quiet atmosphere in the setting and for the reading of this story. However, Easter joy should not be contained! After reading the story, teach the children to sing "Alleluia!" with a melody you are familiar with. After a couple of verses of this, hand out rhythm instruments, especially bells. Lead a parade through your classroom or home, still singing and letting children enjoy the music they are making with the instruments. End at the snack table, where a festive table has been set. Use flowers and colorful placemats. Provide a snack that is more bountiful and more celebrative than usual. And enjoy the feast!

Project Checklist

Easter at a Glance

Easter

And entering the tomb, they saw a young man sitting on the right side, dressed in a white robe; and they were amazed. And he said to them, "Do not be amazed; you seek Jesus of Nazareth, who was crucified. He has risen, he is not here; see the place where they laid him. But go, tell his disciples and Peter that he is going before you to Galilee; there you will see him, as he told you." Mark 16:5-7

Easter is the highest and holiest of days for all Christians. It is a day we celebrate the new life we have in Jesus, Son of God, who died and three days later rose from the dead. The gift of hope and life after death is the eternal message of the day. What a sacrifice Jesus made for each and everyone of us!

Easter Sunday is celebrated on a different calendar date each year. It falls on the first Sunday after the first full moon of spring. Easter Sunday cannot fall on a Sunday before March 22 or after April 25. The first Nicene Council in A.D. 325 established this formula for determining the date of Easter. Ash Wednesday and the beginning of Lent fall 40 days before Easter.

Scholars and historians have different ideas about where the word Easter came from. Some say that it comes from the English word "Eastre," which was the name of the pagan goddess of spring and new life. Others say it comes from the German word "eostarun," which means dawn. Dawn would relate to the time of day Jesus rose from the dead. Still others believe that the word Easter comes from the Latin word "albae," which means dawn and white. White is the color of purity and the color of clothes the newly baptized wore on Easter.

Prayer

Alleluia! Alleluia! Christ has risen! What a wonderful day this is! On this Easter day we celebrate with joy and hope in our hearts. Jesus our Lord has risen! Be with us today, Lord Jesus, as we celebrate with family and friends the Good News of Easter. In the name of the Father, and of the Son, and of the Holy Spirit. Amen.

Activities
Easter and New Life

When talking with the children about Easter make connections between the New Life we have in Jesus and his resurrection and springtime and the new life we see in nature. Discuss the symbols of flowers, eggs and baby animals. Look at the trees and grass and talk about how they begin to turn green and grow in the spring! Be sure to continue Easter celebrations in the days and weeks that follow Easter Sunday.

Family Traditions

Share family traditions for celebrating Easter.

Basket Blessings

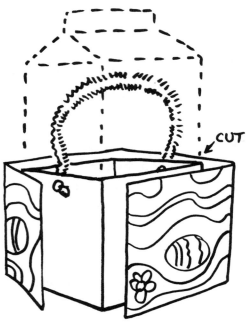

Many years ago Christians had the tradition of having their Easter baskets blessed on Easter Sunday. Families would bring a basket containing the food for their holiday dinner to church for the priest to bless. The baskets were brought to the altar before Mass and then taken home at the end. Make up mini-Easter baskets for the children. Cut the top off of individual sized milk cartons and cover the bottom in festive wrapping paper. Add a pipe cleaner handle and some Easter grass. Fill the baskets with a few sweet treats, a prayer card and small toy. During Easter week, the week following Easter, invite your pastor to visit to bless the baskets before the children take them home. Gather in your prayer space or go to the altar of your church. Use the following ideas.

Have the children place their baskets near or on the altar. Gather the children around the baskets.

Prayer

In the Name of the Father and the Son and the Holy Spirit. We pray, Alleluia! Alleluia! Today we gather together to continue our Easter Celebration with the blessing of these baskets. Legends of the past tell us that the use of baskets came from the symbol of the bird nest. A bird nest holds the eggs out of which new life, new baby birds come. What a good symbol this is of Jesus coming out of the dark tomb of death to new life.

Blessing

Dear Lord, we ask your blessing for these wonderful, faith-filled children gathered together during this Easter season. Keep them always in your loving care. Bless these baskets filled with goodies, reminders of the life-giving gift we received through the resurrection of your Son, Jesus. Amen.

Liturgical Color

The Easter Season color is white reminding us of victory and joy.

Easter Traditions

Easter Eggs

German people long ago wrote the names of each child and their
birthday on dyed eggs as part of their Easter observance. With
permanent marker have the children write their names and birthday
on large plastic eggs. Decorate the rest of the egg with stickers or
sequins. Place a copy of the Easter prayer above or a short blessing in
the egg and send home.

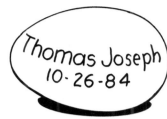

Tree Trimming

Bring in a tree branch from outside and put it in a vase or jar.
Provide the children with egg shaped cutouts of many different sizes
and colors. Have the children decorate the paper eggs using markers,
glitter, yarn, ribbon etc. After the eggs have dried, punch a hole in the
top of them and lace ribbon through the hole for hanging. Place the
eggs on the branches and enjoy throughout the Easter season.

Easter Hare

What does a rabbit have to do with Easter? In pre-Christian times, a Germanic spring goddess
had a hare as her messenger. As the hare is a noble animal with characteristics that symbolize
Jesus, it became a Christian symbol: Like Jesus, the hare is gentle, never harming anyone; it has
ever-sensitive ears, like Jesus who listened to everyone in need; despite its gentle ways, it has
many enemies; and the wild hare is known to sacrifice itself for the life of another hare.

The Fourth Sunday of Easter – Good Shepherd Sunday

Celebrate Good Shepherd Sunday with a story, a finger play, and a child's version of Psalm 23.

God Watches Over Us

Jesus was a storyteller. Once he told a story to help us understand how he watches over us
and loves us. Here is that story:

Story: The Good Shepherd

A man who had many sheep took them out to a large field to eat. He watched them carefully.
If one got caught on a bush, he would hurry over to untangle it. If another hurt its leg, he would
clean and bandage it.

When it rained, he pulled his cloak up over his head, but he stayed with his sheep. When it
was dark, he did not sleep. If the wind blew at his cloak, making him shiver, he still watched over
his sheep.

This shepherd protected them because he knew that wild animals could come to hurt the sheep. He watched because he knew some could wander off and get lost. He guarded them because he loved them.

One gusty day, the shepherd counted his sheep—97, 98, 99, only 99? He was supposed to have 100! One was missing.

He left the other sheep, wrapped his cloak around himself and hurried off to find the lost sheep. He searched through bushes and behind boulders. He hurt his hand on thorns. The wind tore at his clothes. Then it began to rain, but he kept looking for that one sheep.

Finally he found it behind a large rock. It was a small lamb, its fleece wet and matted with dirt. It had injured its leg and could not walk.

Gently, the shepherd picked up the lamb, carefully so as not to hurt it. He placed it on his shoulders for the long walk home. As he drew closer, he called to his friends, "Come and celebrate with me! I have found the sheep that I had lost!"

Jesus told us this story because he is like that good shepherd.

Fingerplay

Once there was a man who had a big flock of sheep. (EXTEND ARMS TO SHOW "BIG")

He watched over them day and night. (PUT HAND TO FOREHEAD AS IF GAZING OUT AT FLOCK)

One day he counted the sheep. (POINT, AS IF COUNTING)

One was missing! (HOLD UP ONE FINGER)

The shepherd looked to the left (TURN TO THE LEFT), and to the right. (TURN TO THE RIGHT)

He looked up (LOOK UP) and he looked down. (LOOK DOWN)

Then he found the sheep! Gently he carried it back home.

(CIRCLE ARMS AS IF CARRYING A BABY)

That is how Jesus is. He watches over us (EXTEND ARMS OUT, PALMS UP) and loves us all. (BRING ARMS IN TO HUG SELF)

Prayer

The Lord is my shepherd,
I shall not want.
Surely goodness and mercy
shall follow me
all the days of my life.

Ascension of the Lord

"But you shall receive power when the Holy Spirit has come upon you; and you shall be my witness in Jerusalem and in all Judea and Samaria and to the end of the earth." And when he had said this, as they were looking on, he was lifted up, and a cloud took him out of their sight."
Acts 1: 8,9

Christ's Ascension is a mystery of faith, just as is his Incarnation and Resurrection. Something happened between Jesus' bodily rising from the dead and the time when humans no longer physically saw him in their presence, but we cannot fully understand what that was. St. Luke describes the Ascension at the end of his gospel and again at the beginning of the Acts of the Apostles, though his descriptions vary in detail.

The Ascension of the Lord always falls on the 40th day after Easter, which is a Thursday. In many dioceses, this important feast is now celebrated on the following Sunday. Ascension literally means to go up, and on this day we commemorate the earthly body of Jesus going up to heaven. Jesus and his disciples were on the Mount of Olives near Jerusalem. He told his followers that soon they would receive the power of the Holy Spirit, and then it would be up to them to spread the Good News of his Resurrection to the rest of the world. An angel appeared after Jesus ascended and promised that Jesus would someday return.

Prayer

Today we are reminded of the new life we have in Jesus. Before going up to heaven, Jesus told His disciples that the Holy Spirit would soon come and then it would be up to them to spread the word of God. Help us to spread the Good News about the life of Jesus by thinking of others first and always doing our best. In Jesus' name we pray. Amen.

Story: Jesus Forever (Based on Acts 1:6-11)

Ascension is part of the Easter celebration, and therefore important that children become aware of the Scripture that tells the story. Help them come to see that it was not a sad leave-taking, but a time when the apostles more fully understood that Jesus was God, and that he would forever be with them. And it means he is forever with us. It is cause for rejoicing!

Jesus had risen from the dead forty days before. Now he was in the city of Jerusalem with his apostles. "You will go out to many lands and teach people all that I have taught you," Jesus said to them. "God will send the Holy Spirit to guide you. You will go to the ends of the earth."

Then he was lifted up, and a cloud covered him so the apostles could no longer see Jesus. Two angels appeared. "Why do you look for Jesus?" they asked. "He has been taken from you into heaven, but he will return."

And so, his apostles understood that Jesus would always be with them, even though they could no longer see him.

As this story is one we receive in faith, it is best perceived through symbol. Offer children symbols of the Ascension without explaining them. Allow the symbols to speak to each child's heart.

Celebration Table Ideas

On the Celebrations table, place a green cloth representing the earth. Scatter glitter and stars on it, and add a bouquet of flowers. The stars on the green cloth show the connection we now have between heaven and earth because of Jesus' Ascension. The flowers show that Jesus' words and works are flowering even now, on earth.

Activities
Cloud Watching
Take spring walks and admire the clouds. Enjoy their movements, their interplay with the sun, their subtle colors during the daytime.

Cloud Painting
Offer large sheets of paper for painting. Offer only blue and white paint.

Pentecost
"And suddenly a sound came from heaven like the rush of a mighty wind, and it filled all the house where they were sitting. And there appeared to them tongues as of fire, distributed and resting on each one of them. And they were all filled with the Holy Spirit and the Spirit gave them utterance." Acts 2:2-4

Pentecost is celebrated 50 days or the 7th Sunday after the Resurrection of Jesus on Easter. The word Pentecost means fifty. The name Pentecost also comes from the Greek name for the Festival of Shavuoth, which is a Jewish festival of thanksgiving celebrated 50 days after Passover. On this day, we remember that Mary, a couple of other women, and the twelve disciples were in the upper room of a house in Jerusalem. As they prayed together a strong wind came up with a loud noise and flames of fire came to rest above the heads of the twelve disciples. Immediately the disciples were inspired and filled with courage and strength to spread the word of God to all people.

The gifts of the Holy Spirit are knowledge, understanding, counsel, strength, piety, fear of the Lord and wisdom. The fruits of the Holy Spirit are love, peace, joy, patience, kindness, goodness, faithfulness, generosity, mildness, self-control, modesty and chastity.

The dove, wind and fire are all symbols of the Holy Spirit.

Liturgical Color: Red
Red is the color used for vestments and decorations in the church this day.

Prayer
On this day of Pentecost, we are thankful for the gift of the Holy Spirit. Just as the disciples were empowered to share the Good News of Jesus, so too are we. We pray that the Fruits of the Holy Spirit, love, peace, joy, patience, kindness, goodness, faithfulness, generosity, mildness, self-control, modesty and chastity, will come to grow in us as we grow in our love for you, God. May the Holy Spirit be with us. Amen.

The Celebration Table and Activity
Pentecost is the great celebration of Christian community. Your table can serve to illustrate this with a beautiful ritual. If possible, display an illustration of the Holy Spirit descending on Mary and the apostles. The tablecloth should be red or white. Place a large white candle on the table, surrounded by smaller white candles, enough for each person in the home or classroom.

Add white flowers, such as daisies. Point out to children that the daisy is made up of individual petals, all connected to a single center point, as are Christians from all over the world connected to Christ.

When the family or class is assembled, light the big candle, explaining that it is the light of Christ. Then have each person light a candle to represent himself. Read the Pentecost story together.

Repeat the candle lighting on different days, adding candles. Children can choose to light candles for relatives or friends, and for those who have died. In this way, they begin to understand the community of saints, our connectedness with all others, near and far, past and present, who are Christians.

Activities

Fruit of the Spirit Board

Make a bulletin board illustrating the Fruits of the Spirit. Use block letters for the title of the bulletin board, "Fruit of the Spirit." Write these words on cards or cutouts of fruit and tack to the board. Have the children look for magazine pictures that go with each gift. Add drawings, or other cutouts.

Fruit on Fruit

Collect artificial or plastic fruit and write one fruit of the spirit on each. Place these in a basket near your prayer center. During prayer time have each child take a turn choosing one piece of fruit and then talk about its meaning.

Spirit as Wind

Sometimes the Holy Spirit is compared to the wind. We can feel it, see and hear its effects, but we cannot actually see it. Talk about the effects of the wind. We see laundry, flags, windmills, tree branches, leaves and kites blow in the wind. The wind catches the sail on a sailboat and makes it go.

Kites

Make kites from construction paper and add a long piece of yarn to the end. Using the pattern provided write the name of each gift on a knot cut out and staple them to the tail of the kite. On the front of the kite write, "Gifts of the Spirit." Add a piece of yarn to the top of the kite for hanging.

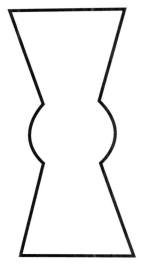

Pentecost Traditions

In some Christian countries, Pentecost is also known as "Whitsun" or White Sunday. The image of the white dove representing the Holy Spirit, and the newly baptized donning white gowns, has resulted in a tradition of people wearing white that day. In northern Europe, many white blossoms are in bloom at this time, and they are included in any decorating. A cake with white icing is often served.

Pentecost comes in springtime. There is a custom on this day to gather green branches and "decorate" a person with the branches. This person is called "Green George" or "Leaf Man." This disguised person hides and children try to find the Leaf Man in a game called "hunting the green man."

Project Checklist

_____

_____

_____

_____

_____

_____

_____

_____

_____

_____

_____

_____

_____

April at a Glance

Dedication for April: The Holy Spirit or The Holy Eucharist and Celebration Table Ideas
April's Liturgical Colors
Patron Saints of the Month
April 1: April Fools' Day
April 22: Arbor Day / Earth Day
April 23: St. George
April 25: St. Mark the Evangelist
April 29: Catherine of Siena
April 30: St. Walpurgis' Night

Dedication for April: The Holy Spirit or The Holy Eucharist and Celebration Table Ideas

This dedication recognizes two ways in which God is present in our everyday lives.

Celebration Table Ideas

Use the Celebration Table to help the children focus on the importance of the Holy Eucharist. Once Lent is over, cover the table with a white cloth. Place a loaf of bread and a cup of juice on the table. You may also want to include a children's Bible and a resurrection cross or picture of Jesus.

April's Liturgical Colors

Lent: Purple

Purple is used during the 40 days of Lent to symbolize penance and sacrifice.

Easter: White

The Easter Season color is white reminding us of victory and joy.

Patron Saints of the Month

April 7: John the Baptist De La Salle: teachers
April 23: George: Greece, England, Portugal, soldiers, farmers, fruit tree growers, gardeners, boy scouts, springtime
April 25: Mark: Venice, notaries
April 29: Catherine of Siena: Italy, nursing services, fire protection

April 1 – April Fools' Day

We are fools on Christ's account. Ah, but in Christ you are wise. 1 Corinthians 4:10

No one is exactly sure how the fun of April Fools' day was started but there are a couple of theories. One is that April 1 occurs in the spring when the weather is changing. Mother Nature is fooling everyone with warmer, longer days and the beginnings of new life. The second theory has to do with the change in the Gregorian calendar. In 1582 King Charles IX, along with the Church, changed the beginning of the year to January 1 instead of April 1. At that time, March 25 began a week of merriment, which included parties and gift giving (probably similar to what we do today) which ended on April 1, the first day of the new year. When the change in calendar came about, many people were either unaware or not interested in going along with the change. The other problem was getting the word out to all of Europe that there had been a change. As a result the people who were slow to change were sending gifts and celebrating at the wrong time and hence were called fools. Eventually the people who were celebrating on the correct day started playing tricks on those who weren't on April 1. Common tricks of the time were scheduling parties that didn't exist and sending people on errands that weren't necessary. It didn't take long for the term "April Fools" to take hold in reference to the uninformed souls of the time.

Prayer

Being a fool for you, Jesus, is the best kind of fool to be. Following Jesus when others may think us foolish is what we are asked to do. We are happy knowing that Jesus is in our hearts and with us when we work and play and have fun! As we laugh and "fool" around today, we do so knowing that Jesus is right there with us. In the name of Jesus we pray. Amen.

Activities
Foolish Discussion

Share a bit of the history surrounding April Fools Day. Talk about playing a few good-natured tricks at home and school.

Playing Fools

If your class is really enthused about this day you might want to set time limits on the foolery. Set a timer and let the children know that they can joke and play tricks until the timer rings and then it is time to get back on track.

Joke Sharing

Ask each child to bring in a joke from home that could be shared at gathering time. Put the jokes together in a class joke book. Make copies and send the class joke book home.

A Bit of Fools

Color the milk with food coloring at snack time. Place gummy worms on crackers or in applesauce or pudding.

Turn things upside down or inside out for the day. Have everything done before the children arrive and see if they notice the changes. Turn the tables sideways, the chairs backward, etc. Wear your own clothes backwards or inside out. Put your glasses on the back of your head, etc. Change the schedule or location of certain activities. Try to play baseball with a basketball or soccer with a football.

Put out some fall or Christmas decorations or plan an art project that doesn't go with this time of year.

Potato Art

Make foolish looking potato heads using real potatoes and other sliced vegetables. Give each child a potato and other sliced vegetables such as celery, radishes, carrots, and broccoli and have them use the smaller vegetables to make facial features, etc. Cut toothpicks in half to attach the features to the face. Use parsley and leaves from the celery for hair. Send the potatoes home with the above prayer.

April 22 – Arbor Day / Earth Day

"Bless the Lord, O my soul! O Lord my God, thou art very great ! The trees of the Lord are watered abundantly, the cedars of Lebanon which he planted." Psalms 104: 1,16,17

In the 1840s Julius Sterling Morton settled with his family in the Nebraska Territory. The lack of trees had an impact on them, as there was not wood for building, fuel and shade in the hot dry summers. As time went on Morton made tree planting in Nebraska his mission. As the Nebraska territory grew, Morton became State Secretary and proposed a plan to establish an Arbor Day on which everyone in the state would plant trees. The idea was very popular and on April 10, 1872, one million trees were planted. After Morton died the state of Nebraska declared Arbor Day a legal holiday and changed it to April 22, which was Morton's birthday.

Most states in the U.S. celebrate Arbor Day on April 22. However, depending on the climate, this day may be different in different states. For example, Hawaii celebrates its Arbor Day in November, which is a better time for planting.

Almost 100 years later, this country saw a huge environmental movement develop and Arbor Day was also named Earth Day. Gaylord Nelson, a senator from Wisconsin introduced this day as one to increase awareness of the environmental issues of modern times. All over the country rallies, workshops, seminars, etc. were held to make people aware of the problems of pollution to the air and water and the depletion of our natural resources. The day was a huge success in that 200 million people across the country participated in some manner. Since that time April 22 has been a day to educate and inform and actively participate in taking care of our earth.

Prayer

Dear Lord, you created this wonderful planet we live on. Thank you for the gifts of air, water, trees, animals, birds and an abundance of other natural resources. As we think about Arbor Day and Earth Day, we ask you to help us be good consumers of all that is in our world. We will do our best to put trash where it belongs, waste as little water and other natural resources as possible. We will also do our best to take care of our toys and clothes so that they can be used and reused. We pray this in our Creator's name. Amen.

Activities
Recycling Discussion
Talk about the environment and how important it is to take care of our earth. Brainstorm with the children about the kinds of things can we do at home and school. How can we conserve water and resources? What is recycling? Are there things we are not recycling now that we could start recycling?

School/Community Recycling
Check with the rest of your staff and see if there are ways to recycle more or save resources in your building. Implement these ideas with the children.

Picking up Trash
Plan a nature walk and give everyone a brown grocery bag to put trash in. If possible go around the block or a little farther out in the community to pick up trash.

Recycle Art
Use recycled items to make sculptures or other projects.

Posters
Have each of the children make a poster promoting Earth Day or Arbor Day. Display these in a hallway or lobby for all to see.

Planting Trees
Check with your local forestry office and find out if there are free trees available to plant on Arbor Day. Or collect change from the families in your program and buy a tree to plant on your church grounds. Be sure to have a little ceremony and prayer after planting. As time goes on decorate the tree and make it your own. Hang bird feeders on the tree; string popcorn and cranberries on it at Christmas time and in the spring add a birdhouse or two.

April 23 – St. George
St. George was most likely a soldier in the fourth century. He was a Christian who was very open about his faith. He was martyred under the persecution orchestrated by the emperor, Diocletian. Two centuries later, George had become a mythical figure. His status as soldier lent itself to stories of him fighting a fearsome dragon. Dragons have long been symbols of evil and slaying them is an allegory for the victory of good over evil. Christians used this allegory to

portray Christ's victory over evil.

The most famous story tells of George entering a town where a dragon had been eating farm animals and had now moved onto devouring the townspeople. Just as the king's daughter was about to be caught by the dragon, George arrived, drew his sword and slew the enemy. In his gratitude, the king offered him great riches, but instead, George opted for a promise for churches to be built and the poor ministered to.

Activity: *St. George and the Dragon*

A most remarkable picture book, readily available in libraries, is *Saint George and the Dragon*, adapted by Margaret Hodges, illustrated by Trina Schart Hyman (Little, Brown and Company, 1984). The text is full of imagery, presenting themes of goodness, courage, tenacity, purity, evil and fear in a rich tapestry of words. The illustrations are magnificent and match the drama and beauty of the story. Bring this book into your home or classroom and enjoy sharing it. You will probably be asked to read it more than once! Then offer children drawing paper and markers or paints and suggest they do their own illustration of this celebrated story.

April 25 – St. Mark the Evangelist

Mark is one of the writers of the four Gospels. He was not an apostle, but a member of the first group of Christians. It is believed that Mark's mother opened her house as a place of prayer while St. Peter was imprisoned. Mark also traveled with St. Paul, acting as his secretary. Most likely, much of his Gospel was based on information from St. Peter. Mark wrote for a variety of people, so his writing is simple and direct.

Discussion Starter: Whom did St. Mark travel with?

April 29 – Catherine of Siena

Catherine lived a very long time ago in the city of Siena, in Italy. She had 24 older brothers and sisters! When she was seven years old, she decided she would work for God when she grew up. As a young woman, she spent many hours praying. Sometimes she prayed so hard, she heard and saw Jesus! A few years later, she began a different kind of work for God. Catherine visited prisoners and helped sick people. She talked with people who had done wrong things, helping them to see how they could stop. She wrote hundreds of letters to help people with problems. Catherine showed people how to settle fights over land. She even helped the pope. Catherine is remembered as one of our smartest and greatest saints.

Discussion Starter: Whom did Catherine visit?

April 30 – St. Walpurgis' Night

Long, long ago, people in Europe believed there were only two seasons: the cold and the warm. They also believed that May 1st was the start of the warm season and November 1st was the start of the cold season. This gave them a big worry. They thought that at midnight on the eves of those dates, when the two seasons met there was small crack between them and good and bad spirits could slip through and come to their houses!

What could they do? Some people in Austria stuck brooms, rakes and other tools upside down in the ground. They hoped these could catch any bad spirits flying by! Others in Sweden built big fires to scare off any bad spirits.

It just happens that a saint has her feast day on April 30, one of these "scary" days. Her name was Walpurgis. She was an English nun who opened convents in Germany. She studied medicine and was often able to cure sicknesses. When she died, people thought of her as a saint. Soon they connected her feast day with the night of spirits, even though she had nothing to do with this. Even today, some Swedish people light bonfires on St. Walpurgis' Night, but this is not to ward off ghosts, but to welcome spring and celebrate her memory!

Discussion Starter: Why do people in Sweden often light bonfires on St. Walpurgis' feast day?

Project Checklist

_____
_____
_____
_____
_____
_____
_____
_____
_____
_____
_____
_____
_____
_____

May at a Glance

Dedication for May: Mary
Patron Saints of the Month
May's Liturgical Colors
May Altars, Celebration Table Ideas, Crowning
May 1: May Day
May 3: St. James and St. Philip, Apostles
Second Sunday of May: Mother's Day
May 14: St. Matthias, Apostle
Saints and Traditions of Springtime Planting
May 11-15: Three Freezing Saints, Rogation Days, and St. Isadore the Farmer
May 15: St. Isadore and Maria
May 17: St. Josephine Bakhita
May 26: St. Philip Neri
May 30 (Traditional): Memorial Day

Dedication for May: Mary

We dedicate this lovely month to Mary, the Mother of God, and the mother of us all.

Patron Saints of the Month

May 1: Joseph the Worker: workers, as well as others listed in March
May 15: Isadore and his wife, Maria Torribia: farmers, laborers, rural life in the United States

May's Liturgical Colors

Easter Season: White

The liturgical color used is white, the color of joy and victory.

Ordinary Time: Green

The liturgical color used is green, the color of hope and life.

May Altar, Celebration Table, Crowning

A sweet folk custom is the May altar, which is simply a way to show that Mary is very loved by us. On the Celebration Table, place a statue of Mary on a pretty cloth, preferably in white or blue. Place fresh flowers there throughout the month.

Activities
May Crowning
Create a simple crown that will fit the statue's head using tiny silk roses on wire stems. Place a water-filled but otherwise empty vase by the statue. Gather around the table, and give each child a small fresh flower. Say a "Hail Mary" together, then reverently place the crown onto the statue's head. Have each child place a flower into the vase.

Ladybug Birdbath
In the Middle Ages the ladybug was dedicated to Mary and called the "beetle of our Lady." It is thought that the bug's cute appearance and help in controlling pests for the farmers led to their honor. Make a ladybug birdbath for your church garden in honor of Mary. Purchase a 12-14" clay saucer and an 8-10" clay pot. Turn the pot upside down. Have each child in the class leave a fingerprint made from red acrylic paint on the side of the pot. After the paint

dries, have the children draw spots and a head with a fine point permanent marker on the red ladybug. The children should also sign their names near their bug. On the rim of the clay saucer write "Hail Mary, Pray for Us," again in permanent marker. Seal the outside of the ladybug pot and rim with clear glaze or varnish. Find a place in your church garden to put the birdbath and fill with water.

May 1 – May Day
Historically May 1 has been a day to celebrate spring. People celebrated with May Poles, flowers, baskets and other festivities. Since the 1880s May Day in other parts of the world has been a day to celebrate the labor movement. Canada, the U.S. and Bermuda are the only countries to observe Labor Day in September.

May Day in the U.S. was proclaimed Law Day in 1958, however most Americans think of the day as a celebration of spring. Traditionally children make baskets, fill them with goodies and give them away.

In France, May is the month of the Virgin Mary. In honor of Mary, the French crown young girls as May queens who then lead processions through the streets.

Prayer
Lord, we thank you for the warm weather, the flowers and trees that are bursting with new growth. We ask you to bless us as we celebrate May Day. Amen.

Activity: *May Day Baskets*
Use up left over envelopes to make may baskets. Seal the envelop (that is square or almost square), and cut about 1/4" off the top fold with a decorative scissors. Punch a hole on each side of the envelope and lace a ribbon through each one for hanging. Decorate the sides of the basket with

stickers or drawings by the children. Fill the baskets with candy, tea bags or other goodies for seniors in your community. Add a note that reads, "God bless you on May Day."

May 3 – St. James and St. Philip, Apostles

These two saints were Jesus' apostles who worked hard in the early days of the Church. James was the son of Alphaeus, not the James who was the brother of John and son of Zebedee. Today's saint is sometimes called "James the Less," not a particularly complimentary name to us. This was probably due to the fact that he was younger than the other James who is called "James the Greater." Some say he was also known as "James the Just." It is believed that he became the bishop of Jerusalem, and that he wrote the Letter of James in the New Testament. From that, we can learn that St. James was very concerned that in the Christian Church, poor and rich people were treated alike and fairly. He also worried that Christians must remember that Jesus wants us to help others.

St. Philip brought his friend Nathaneal to meet Jesus. Later, he and St. Andrew brought a group of Greek people to meet him. Philip must have been very enthusiastic about Jesus! He was also with Jesus at the miracle of the loaves and fishes. Perhaps he was also a practical man, for he told Jesus it would take six months' wages to buy enough food to feed 5,000 people. Quick thinking!

Discussion Starters: How did St. James want the poor to be treated? What miracle did Philip see?

Second Sunday of May – Mother's Day

"But Mary kept all these things, pondering them in her heart." Luke 2:19

Mother's Day was first observed in 1907. Anna Jarvis of Philadelphia asked her church to have a special service in memory of her mother on the anniversary of her mother's death. By 1914 a presidential proclamation was made naming Mother's Day as the second Sunday of May. It wasn't long before the tradition began of wearing a white carnation if your mother was dead and a colored carnation if your mother was alive.

Prayer

On this Mother's Day, we thank you, dear Lord, for the mothers in our lives. We are grateful for and treasure all of the women in our lives that love us and care for us. Not only do we remember our mothers, but our grandmothers, godmothers, aunts and sisters and friends. In the name of your Holy Mother Mary, we pray. Amen.

Activities
Mom Discussion

Talk to the children about mothers. Be sensitive to the fact that some of the children do not live with their moms. Ask the children about all the things their mothers or the other special women in their lives do for them. Why do they do all those things? How can we show those special women our love and appreciation for them? Remind the children that Jesus' Mother, Mary, was very important to him.

Mother's Day Cards

Make a Mother's Day card for the children to give to their moms or other special women in their lives. Write a message of love in the middle of an origami creation that serves as its own card, gift box and envelope. Cut construction paper into 9" squares. Have the children draw a picture and write a Mother's Day message on one side of the square. Fold the paper diagonally across the middle of the square. The drawing should be inside the fold. Lay the paper triangle in front of you with the fold towards your lap. The fold will measure 13" in length. Mark the fold at 4 1/4th" and 8 1/2". Fold each side point to the center making the crease at the 4 1/4th" and 8

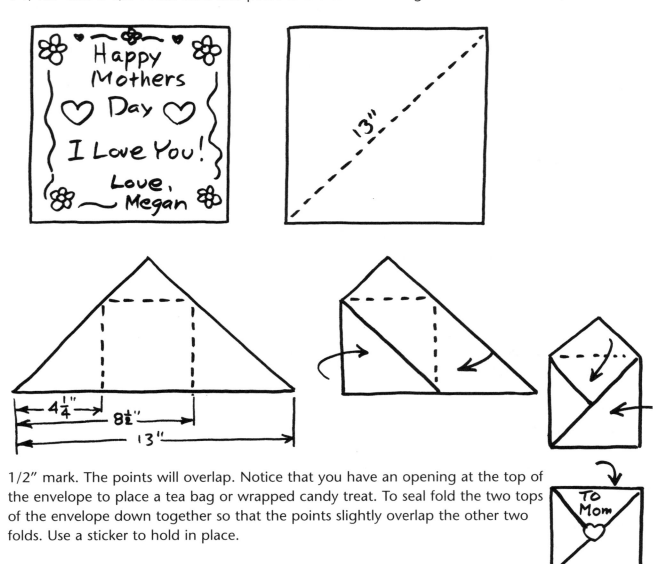

1/2" mark. The points will overlap. Notice that you have an opening at the top of the envelope to place a tea bag or wrapped candy treat. To seal fold the two tops of the envelope down together so that the points slightly overlap the other two folds. Use a sticker to hold in place.

Mother's Day Pots
Paint clay flowerpots with acrylic paint and plant seeds or a small bedding plant in it.

Mother's Day Banners
Make a Mother's Day banner. Cut muslin into 10" by 14" pieces. Fold over the top about 1" and hold in place with strip of masking tape laid end to end. This will make a casing for a dowel. If you have enough help a sewn casing gives a more finished edge. Have the children leave a handprint with paint on the center of the banner. When the paint has dried add a Mother's Day greeting and the child's name. Place an 11" to 12" dowel in the casing and tie a ribbon to the ends of it for hanging.

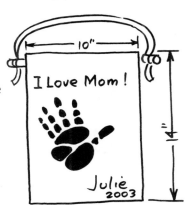

Mother's Day Bracelets
Make Mother's Day bracelets with the children for their moms. Coordinate the beads and use the following poem. Make copies of the poem on card stock and have the children sign their names to the cards.

To Mom on Mother's Day
This little bracelet was made with love for you on this Mother's Day,
The beads were strung to show you what you mean to me in oh so many ways.
The red is for the love you give to me each and every day.
Purple is for the fun we have when we laugh and play.
Green is for how much I've grown with your tender care.
How wonderful it is for me to know that you're always there.
Blue is for how good I feel when you tuck me in at night.
And yellow's for the joy I feel seeing you in the morning light.
Pink is for folding hands and teaching me how to pray,
And warmly, gently, lovingly, showing me God's way.
This little bracelet was made with love for you on this Mother's Day.
The beads were strung to show you what you mean to me in oh so many ways.
I love you Mom!

May 14 – St. Matthias, Apostle
Matthias was a follower of Jesus, but not one of the original 12 apostles. However, after Jesus had ascended into heaven and Judas Iscariot, one of the twelve, had died, St. Peter called the eleven apostles together to choose a new apostle. They wanted to keep the number at 12, since that number symbolized the complete family of God. Matthias had seen Jesus' miracles and had learned Jesus' teachings, so he was chosen.

Discussion Starter: Why was Matthias chosen?

May 11-15 – Saints and Traditions of Springtime Planting
Three Freezing Saints, Rogation Days, and St. Isadore the Farmer

SS. Mamertus, Pancras and Servatus are known as the Three Freezing Saints. They are also called the Ice Saints and the Frost Saints. They got these unusual names because of the thinking that these saints might come to play a trick on people by bringing a frost. After the days of the Three Freezing Saints are over, it was believed that it was safe to plant more tender plants like tomatoes. There is no reason to think these saints, all holy people, had any bad feelings about farmers. In fact, St. Mamertus began a custom called Rogation Days just for such people.

Rogation Days

In the fifth century, Archbishop Mamertus began a custom of prayer and processions, asking God to protect crops, orchards, and animals. People walked around fields, singing psalms. These days of prayer are called "rogation" because the Latin word "rogare" means "to ask." Hundreds of years later, it was decided that rogation days would be kept at times when a bishop feels a special need for prayer and will ask people to keep a rogation day.

Discussion Starters: What did people think the Three Freezing Saints might do? What does the Latin word "rogare" mean?

May 15 – St. Isadore and Maria
An American Rogation Day

The feast day of St. Isadore the Farmer has become a rogation day in many parts of the United States. With the encouragement of the Catholic Rural Life Conference, many people gather in different farming communities for a blessing of the farmers and their lands, asking God to bless the year's crops in remembrance of St. Isadore and his good wife, Maria, who had a great love of God and a respect for God's earth and creatures.

Isadore and Maria were poor, uneducated farmworkers, living in Spain around the 10th century. Their only child died very young, but Maria and Isadore helped many other people who were even poorer than they were, and also protected animals. They were considered very holy people and were loved and respected by many. Here is a story in a booklet of how God showed others that Isadore was a holy man. Copy the booklet for each child, cut and assemble the pages, and read about Isadore and his helpers.

Booklet Story

[PAGE 1, COVER] Who's Plowing the Field? A Story of St. Isadore

[PAGE 2] Isadore worked hard planting fields. As he worked, he prayed.

[PAGE 3] Isadore loved God's creations: plants, trees, soil and animals. He gave his own food to hungry birds.

[PAGE 4] Isadore always shared his food with people who were hungry, too.

[PAGE 5] Every day, Isadore went to Mass. Sometimes that made him late for work. The other workers complained, "Isadore does not do as much work as we do!"

[PAGE 6] The boss went to watch Isadore. There he saw Isadore, plowing and praying. Then he looked again.

Who's Plowing the Field?

A Story of St. Isadore

[PAGE 7] Who were these others plowing with Isadore? They were angels!

[PAGE 8] Isadore is a very holy man if angels help him with his work!" the boss said. "God must love him very much!"

May 17 – St. Josephine Bakhita

Bakhita was born in a village in Sudan in 1869. When she was only nine years old, she was forced to be a slave. For many years she was treated badly by others. Eventually, she became free and entered a convent. As Sister Josephine, she worked hard and prayed often. She loved God very much. Soon others began to see her goodness, and came to her, asking her to pray for them. She died at age 78. Pope John Paul II canonized her as a saint in October 2000. Bakhita is the first person from Sudan to be canonized.

Discussion Starter: What did Bakhita do when she was freed?

May 26 – St. Philip Neri

Philip Neri was such a jolly little boy that his family called him "Pippo Buono," which is Italian for "Good Little Phil." When he grew up, he still loved to make people laugh. His favorite books were the New Testament and a joke book. He soon found that God planned to use his sense of humor to bring others to God. Philip found a creative way to teach. Finding a group of young men playing ball, Philip would join them, laughing and telling jokes. But then he would say, "Well, friends, when are we going to do good?" Soon he convinced them to visit hospitals and bring food and gifts to poor people. They then came to his meetings, to discuss Bible stories, sing songs, and pray. Many more came to Philip to learn to live as Jesus had taught. And joyful Philip didn't want people to be too serious, or to take him too seriously. Sometimes he had a chipmunk ride on his shoulder! One day, he shaved off half his beard and walked around Rome. He wore a big hat and floppy shoes, and loved to play harmless jokes on people. Hundreds of people came to see the importance of God as well as God's joy in their lives because of Philip.

Discussion Starter: What did Philip have that God chose to use?

May 30 (Traditional) – Memorial Day

"Jesus said, I am the resurrection and the life;
he who believes in me, though he die; yet shall he live,
and whoever lives and believes in me shall never die." John 11:25,26

On Memorial Day we honor all Americans who gave their lives for their country. Flags fly at half-mast and flowers and flags are used to decorate the graves of soldiers who died in battle. Memorial Day is also called Decoration Day because of the tradition of decorating the graves of service men and women. This tradition started with the Gettysburg Address during the Civil War.

In modern times Memorial Day is also called Poppy Day. Disabled veterans sell red, paper poppies at this time of year as a fund-raiser and reminder of the sacrifices made by men and women during war. The red color symbolizes bloodshed; and the flower, hope and new life.

In 1971 Memorial Day was declared a federal holiday to be observed on the last Monday in May. Many people remember their other loved ones who have died as well as those who were in the military.

Prayer

On this Memorial Day, we remember the men and women who have died serving our country. We are grateful for the sacrifice they have made. Lord Jesus, we pray that you will always keep these special people in your loving care. Amen.

Activities
Memorial Day Discussion

Discuss Memorial Day with the children in your group. Talk about the ways we remember those who have died, such as visiting the cemetery and leaving flowers. Ask the children about grandparents and other family members who may have died. Remind them that as Christians we believe that people who die have eternal life with God in heaven.

Memorial

Cut out a cross from tag board and write the names of the people the children have mentioned who have died.

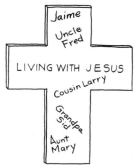

Flagpole Memorial

Tie blooming branches with ribbon around the flagpole as a remembrance for those who have died. Lilacs and other fruit trees are usually flowering at this time.

Memorial Walk

Take a walk in the neighborhood and look for flags that may be half-mast. What other things might you see to remind you that it is Memorial Day? (Flags, parades, poppy sales, etc.)

Victory Gardens

Introduce Victory Gardens to the children. During WWII people were encouraged to grow their own vegetables so that the produce from commercial farmers could go to feed the troops abroad. Growing a Victory Garden was a way to help the country and secure victory. Think about growing a garden of vegetables that could be used to help supply the food pantry at harvest time. Choose a couple of easy things to grow like green beans, cucumbers or squash. Plant and maintain the garden throughout the summer and bring the harvest to the food pantry in the fall.

June at a Glance

Dedication for June: Sacred Heart

June's Liturgical Colors

Patron Saints of the Month

June 3: Charles Lwanga and Companions

June 3: Pope John XXIII, Anniversary of His Death

June 13: St. Anthony of Padua

June 21: First Day of Summer

June 24: St. John the Baptist and Celebration Table Ideas

June 29: St. Peter and St. Paul

The Third Sunday in June: Father's Day

Dedication for June: Sacred Heart

The Sacred Heart, which is Jesus' heart, is a symbol to help us understand that Jesus has a tremendous love for us. It also helps us to remember that Jesus is human as well as God. It was during the years 800 to 1000 that devotion to the Sacred Heart began. One Scripture that especially helps explain this devotion is Jeremiah 31: 31-34: "The human heart, a person's deepest self, is where God has written his covenant."

June's Liturgical Color
Ordinary Time: Green
The liturgical color used is green, the color of hope and life.

Patron Saints of the Month

June 5: Boniface: Germany

June 13: Anthony of Padua: Portugal, travelers, searchers for lost things

June 22: Thomas More: adopted children, lawyers, parents of large families, stepparents

June 3 – Charles Lwanga and Companions

A little more than one hundred years ago, Christianity was begun in the African nation of Uganda. Many of those who became Christian were young men who worked for the king. The king did not want these changes, and he threatened anyone who became Christian. Charles Lwanga and his friends chose to die rather than turn their backs on Jesus. The king thought if these young men died, others would be afraid to become Christian, but he was wrong. Many more began believing in Christ. Today, there are more than six million Christians in Uganda.

Discussion Starter: What did the king do to any one who became a Christian?

June 3 – Pope John XXIII
Anniversary of His Death

Angelo Guiseppe Roncalli grew up with nine brothers and sisters. His family was poor, so he carried his shoes to school so he would not wear them out so soon. When he grew up, he became a priest. Often his work showed him how terrible war is. It also showed him many peoples in many countries. He hoped that the world and its religions could start to work together.

Then he became pope, taking the name John. The first day, he had to wear a cassock that didn't fit him. He thought that was funny! Pope John loved people. He smiled and talked with people. People began to wonder what this new pope would be like.

John was pope for only five years before he died, but in that time his friendliness, and his hope that the world's people could become closer, brought many good changes. He started a very famous meeting, called the Second Vatican Council. Reaching out to people and loving them, as John himself did, became a theme for this very important meeting.

Discussion Starter: What famous meeting did Pope John call together?

June 13 – St. Anthony of Padua

Anthony was a child who grew up with riches, but he chose to live as St. Francis did: in poverty, or poorness, helping others and loving God. One of the gifts God gave Anthony was the ability to teach and give talks. When he was to preach in a church, the church was soon overflowing with people. He also spoke in the town squares, too. People who had done something wrong, like stealing or lying, would make up for it after hearing him speak. He helped many people change their lives. He has become one of the most loved saints of all times.

Tradition

Many people ask St. Anthony to help them find something they have lost. Why? One story tells of Anthony's work on a book of psalms. For years he had been writing it. One day, one of his students, a restless, unhappy young man, took it and ran away. He was going to sell it. Anthony prayed. He wanted his work back, but he was more concerned about the young man. The young man came back, with the book. Anthony helped him to decide what God was calling him to do with his life. Everyone in the monastery felt that Anthony's prayers had found the lost book and the lost young man. They asked him to pray whenever they lost something. Soon people outside of the monastery asked for Anthony's help. And today, many people still pray to him when they lose something.

You may have seen statues or pictures of St. Anthony holding Baby Jesus. There is a story about that too! One time, Anthony was visiting at someone's home. He went outside to pray by himself. He was concentrating on Jesus and talking to him in his heart. Someone looked out the window and saw Anthony in prayer, and had a vision that Anthony was holding Jesus.

June 21 – First Day of Summer

Yours is the day and yours is the night:
You fashioned the moon and the sun.
You fixed all the limits of the land: summer and winter you made.
Psalm 74: 16,17

Summer is the sunniest, warmest time of the year for the Northern Hemisphere of the earth. In the U.S. it is a time of family, vacations and fun.

Prayer

God bless our fun in the sun today,
How great it is to laugh and play.
There are bubbles to blow and bikes to ride,
We are so happy to be able to play outside.
Thank you, dear Lord, for the gifts from above,
Summer is a time we truly love.
Bless us and keep us safe as we play in the sun.
Amen.

Activities

Summer Discussion

Talk with the children about the season of summer. What kinds of things do we do in summer that we can't do at other times? How do we stay safe in the summer? Share plans about how the children will be spending their time.

Ball Toss

Use a beach ball to praise God. Have the children toss the ball back and forth to one another. As each child tosses the ball to someone else, he or she adds a prayer of thanksgiving. Draw a picture of a category of items on each panel of the ball. For example, foods, family, friends, fun, etc. When the children receive the ball they offer a prayer of thanksgiving for an item in the category facing them.

Summer-Time Activities

Plan some fun summer activities such as blowing bubbles, drawing with colored chalk, water balloon toss, or bike parades.

Outside Prayer Corner

Set up your prayer corner in a red wagon and wheel it to different areas outside for prayer time.

Summer Gardens

Plant a class garden. Use paint sticks to label and mark a plant or row of plants for each child. Have the children take turns watering and weeding the garden.

Sand Scoops

Ask parents to send in gallon milk jugs with covers. Cut out the bottom corner of the jug underneath the handle to make a scoop. Decorate the scoops with stickers or drawings with permanent markers. Use them in the sandbox, or for tossing balls or water balloons.

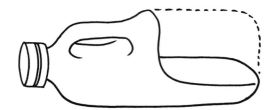

June 24 – St. John the Baptist

St. John the Baptist was a prophet, a person who understands what God wants and tells others so they will know too. Long before Jesus and John the Baptist were born, the prophet Isaiah spoke of them, "See, I am sending my messenger who will prepare you. Listen for the voice of one crying out in the wilderness: 'Prepare the way of the Lord.'" Years and years later, that person, John, did come to prepare the way for Jesus, the Lord.

Story: The Voice in the Wilderness

A man named John lived in the desert. He prayed to understand what job God wanted him to do. Soon he began teaching people. He showed them what they were doing wrong, and told them what they could do to change. More and more people came to hear him, and some asked, "Who are you?"

John said, "I am the voice crying out in the wilderness, as Isaiah said. I am here to tell you to get ready for the Lord who is coming!"

Even more people came to the desert to see John. He took them into the River Jordan to baptize them, to show them that, like water cleaning their bodies, they could clean their souls and become better people.

One day as he was baptizing people, John looked up. There was Jesus, coming toward him! John knew right away that Jesus was the Messiah, the one all the people had been waiting for. Jesus smiled at John and asked to be baptized.

John was amazed. He said, "I should be baptized by you! Why do you come to me?"

Jesus said he wanted to be baptized to show others that they should also be baptized. So John baptized Jesus. As Jesus came out of the water, John saw the Spirit of God come down onto Jesus, and he heard God's voice say, "This is my son, the Beloved, with whom I am well pleased."

John knew he was doing the job God wanted him to do.

Tradition

The feast of John the Baptist is celebrated in different countries in different ways:

• French Canadians have a large festival with street fairs and parades with music and dancing. The streets are decorated with flowers and images of John.

• The Portuguese celebrate with pageants, parades, bullfights and fireworks.

• In England, "Saint John's Tide" is combined with a midsummer celebration. Instead of the date of the summer solstice, they chose June 24. This may be because of the Baptist's words, "He must increase, I must decrease" (John 3:30). John was, of course, referring to Jesus. John's day comes at the time when the sun is beginning to decrease; and six months later, Christmas comes at the time when the sun is beginning to increase. St. John's Tide is a pleasant time of picnics, bonfires and a general appreciation of the gentleness of summer weather and the longer daylight hours.

• In Mexico, the connection between John's work as a baptizer is made with the festivities. "Dia de San Juan" is a significant holiday in Mexico. As John is considered the patron of water, people decorate wells and fountains with flowers and candles. In rural areas, it is traditional to swim in streams and rivers. Bands play and people throw flowers at the swimmers, or flowers are tossed in to float downstream. Celebrations are held at pools in the cities. There are swimming and diving contests. No fancy clothing is worn that day, for one expects to be doused by a bucket of water or thrown into a pool at least once!

Celebration Table

Continue the water theme in a more reverent way at the Celebration Table. Using a light blue tablecloth, add pictures of large bodies of water (a crashing sea, a quiet lake, a powerful waterfall). Place a clear glass pitcher of water in front of the pictures, changing the water regularly to keep it fresh. Add a small vase of fresh flowers.

Activities
Baptism Pictures
Look at pictures of the children's baptisms.

John's Snack
John lived on honey and locusts. Serve snacks with honey, such as fruit sweetened with honey, or bread and honey. Hold the locusts!

Water Play
Celebrate *Dia de San Juan*: Choose a hot day to celebrate. Ask parents to provide children with old clothing that day. Have lots of water play outside: set up a small pool for floating flowers or sailing toy boats; provide a sprinkler for children to run through; bring out small buckets, funnels, and plastic cups to fill with water and dump out; give young sidewalk artists squirt bottles and chalk for picture making; clean paint brushes can be used to paint sidewalks or equipment with water; decorate with flowers; give children dish pans with sudsy water to wash dolls or doll clothes, then hang the clothing on a yarn clothes line; have the children mix juice concentrate with water for snack. In other words, celebrate God's precious gift of water!

June 29 – St. Peter and St. Paul

Hundreds of thousands of people have helped spread Jesus' teaching over the centuries, but these two saints were among the very first, and can be called the "architects" of our faith.

St. Peter was a fisherman, who followed Jesus, learned from him, and loved him. After Jesus was gone from the earth, the other apostles saw him as their leader.

St. Paul had much more education than Peter, and he never met Jesus. At first he was against anyone who believed in Jesus. With God's help, he changed his mind. Then he became a great teacher and organizer of groups of Christians.

Though they were very different men and had different experiences of Jesus, they both used all their energy and talents to bring the news of Jesus to many in the world. They are very great saints and their feast day is celebrated in many countries, including a grand holiday in Rome.

Discussion Starter: What did St. Peter do? What did St. Paul become?

The Third Sunday in June – Father's Day

"For God has commanded, 'honor your father and mother'..." Matthew 15:4

Sonora Smart Dodd of Spokane, Washington, was the catalyst in setting aside a day to honor fathers. The story goes that after hearing a sermon in church regarding Mother's Day, Sonora thought that there needed to be a Father's Day too. She was especially proud of her own father who had raised his six children alone after his wife had died. Sonora promoted the holiday for about a year and in 1910 the city of Spokane celebrated the first Father's Day in the United States. In 1924 the idea was supported by President Calvin Coolidge, but was not made an official national holiday until 1972 when President Nixon signed it into law.

Prayer

Today in our country we honor our fathers. We are thankful for the strength and faith and love we receive from dads everyday. Dear Lord, our heavenly Father, we ask that you bless our dads with good health, happiness and peace all the days of their lives. Thank you for our dads. Amen.

Activities
Dad Discussion
Before going any further with Father's Day activities, ask the children about their dads. Keep in mind that many children do not live with or have a dad. Talk about special friends, grandfathers, uncles, etc. Ask the children why dads and other significant males in their lives are important and special to them. What do we like to do with them? How do they teach us about God?

(Any of the ideas below can be adapted to grandfather, uncle, friend, godfather.)

Father's Day Cards
Enlarge and copy the balloon letters "Dad" (provided on page 161) on a piece of 8 1/2" by 11" paper. In the letters, have the children write words that describe their Dad. Younger children will need help writing. Decorate the rest of the card, roll it (beginning with the short side) and slide it into a paper towel roll. Tie a ribbon around the tube and it is ready to give.

Father's Day Bookmarks

Use 100 or 150 grain sandpaper and cut it into 2 1/2" by 9" pieces. Punch 2 holes at the top of the sandpaper, about 1/2" from the top edge. Lace a piece of rug yarn through the holes. Have the children write "Happy Father's Day" with marker on the piece of sandpaper and sign it from, "One of Your Little Projects" and the child's name.

Bobber Art

Make a bobber necklace or key chain. (Bobbers may be purchased for about fifty cents in a hardware or discount store.) With permanent marker write, "I love Dad" on the bobber. Slip a piece of plastic lace about 18" long through the top of the bobber. (Slip the lace through the same hook on the bobber that the fishing line would go through.) String beads on each side of the bobber and tie the ends together. To make a key chain, use 12" of lace and attach the bobber in the same way as above. Put the two ends of lace together and slip on a few beads. Tie a knot around the last bead and then tie a knot around a silver key ring.

Father's Day Paperweights

Make a paperweight for Dad's desk papers. Take a walk and search for rocks about 3" to 4" in size that have a smooth side. Wash and dry the rocks and with adult help have the children use puffy paint or acrylic paint to write DAD on the smooth side of the rock. After the paint has dried write the child's name and the year on the back of the rock. Spray the top of the rock with clear shellac.

Project Checklist

_____
_____
_____
_____
_____
_____
_____
_____
_____
_____
_____
_____
_____

July

July at a Glance

Dedication for July: Precious Blood

July's Liturgical Color

Patron Saints of the Month

July 3: St. Thomas the Apostle

July 4: Independence Day

July14: Blessed Kateri Tekakwitha and Celebration Table Ideas

July 15: St. Swithun

July 22: St. Mary Magdalene

July 23: St. Bridget of Sweden

July 25: St. James the Apostle

Dedication for July: Precious Blood

We all have blood in our bodies that helps us live. Blood is important, or precious, to us. When Jesus suffered and died for us, he gave up his body and its blood. When we think about all Jesus has done for us, we are thankful that he gave us everything he had to give.

Liturgical Color

Ordinary Time: Green

The liturgical color used is green, the color of hope and life.

Patron Saints of the Month

July 3: Thomas the Apostle: architects and stone cutters, East Indies

July 11: Benedict: Europe

July 23: Bridget of Sweden: Sweden

July 25: James the Greater: Pilgrims

July 26: Anne: Canada, homemakers, women in labor, cabinet makers

July 3 – St. Thomas the Apostle

Thomas was one of the original apostles. There is not much information about him in the Gospels, but we do learn much about the feelings of faith from him. He showed great courage in the story of Lazarus, when the apostles thought they might be in danger. He doubted that the other apostles had seen the risen Jesus. Then, when he saw Jesus himself, he gave us the words that express our belief that Jesus is God. He said to Jesus, "My Lord and my God."

Discussion Starter: Did Thomas at first believe that the other apostles saw the risen Jesus?

July 4 – Independence Day

"We hold these truths to be self evident, that all men are created equal, that they are endowed by their Creator with certain unalienable rights, that among these are Life, Liberty and the pursuit of happiness." Declaration of Independence

Independence Day or the Fourth of July is the birthday of the United States of America. It is the day we celebrate the signing of the Declaration of Independence and the formal breaking of ties with England. The Continental Congress actually met on July 2, 1776 to formally declare independence, but it took two days for them to agree on the language of the document. In 1941 the Fourth of July was declared a federal legal holiday. Declaration Day is always celebrated the 4th. Most communities celebrate this special day with parades, picnics, parties and fireworks in the evening.

Prayer

On this Fourth of July, we thank God for the country we live in. In the United States we can pray to God in any way that we would like. We have opportunities to go to school, to work and to play the games we like to play. Most of all we are able to pray to you, Lord. Today and as we grow older, help us to take care of our country and make it a better place for all people to live. God Bless America! Amen.

Activities
Fourth of July Discussion

Talk a bit about the history of our country. Why did people want to leave their homes to come here to live? What did they think would be better about living in America? Who lived here before the Europeans came to this land? What makes the United States different from other countries? What can we do to make this country stronger? Finally, talk about how the children celebrate this day with their families.

Geography

Put out a large floor puzzle of the U.S. for the children to work on throughout the week. Older children will enjoy talking about the different states and their capitals and the geographic regions of our country.

Flagpole Gathering

Gather around the flagpole for prayer or snack today. Talk about the symbols on the flag and what they represent.

Bicycle Parade

Plan a bike parade. Have the children bring their tricycles and wagons to school and decorate them with red, white and blue crepe paper and balloons, then take a walk around the block. Make paper newspaper hats and give each child an instrument from the rhythm band, and off you go!

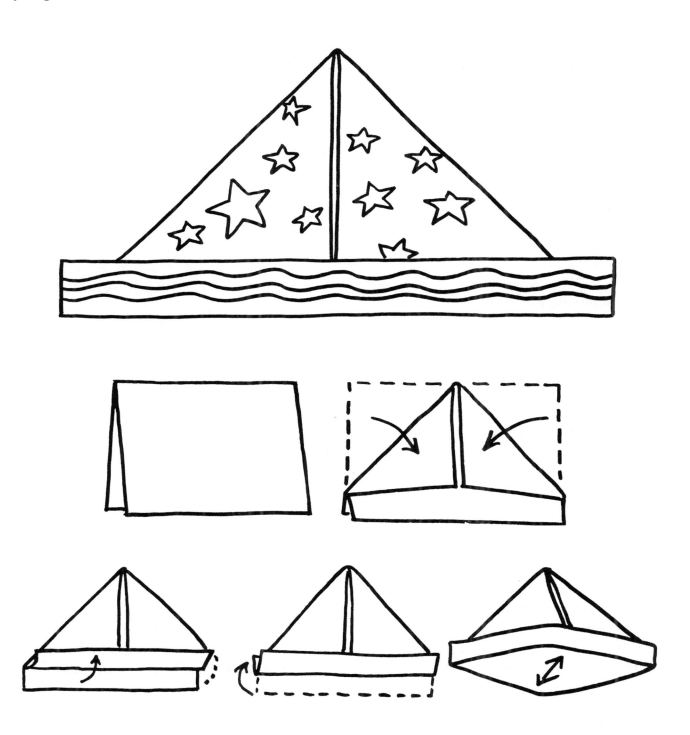

Pompoms

Make a hand full of fireworks for each child. Collect paper towel or toilet tissue rolls for each of the children. Cover them with red, white or blue paper. Patriotic wrapping paper would also work well. Purchase different colors of shredded mylar – the kind used in gift bags or for bows. Take a handful of the mylar and wrap a piece of tape around the bottom of it to hold in place. It will look like a miniature sports pompom. With adult help, fasten the taped end of the mylar bundle to the inside of the tube. Fluff out the top of the mylar to make the fireworks. Use the fireworks for a table decoration to shake during the parade or music making. For older children, attach the mylar pompom to the end of a 12" dowel. Wrap duck tape around the dowel to hold in place.

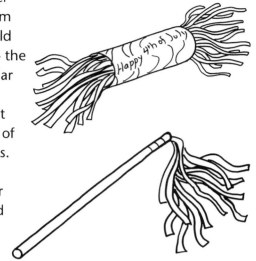

Firework Art

Draw fireworks with colored chalk on black construction paper. Spray the picture with hair spray or shellac to hold the chalk in place.

Hanging Fireworks

Draw with glitter paint, or glue colored mylar strips on large black paper plates to make fireworks. Punch a hole at the top of the plate and lace a ribbon through for hanging. Add a card that says, "God Bless America."

July 14 – Blessed Kateri Tekakwitha

Kateri Tekakwitha (1656-1680) was the first Native American and the first American layperson to be honored with the title of "Blessed," which means she is close to being named a saint.

Her story is written in sections. Give children drawing paper and paints or markers, and have them paint or draw a picture for each section of the story. When finished, combine each child's drawings so each has a finished book.

Story: Child of God in the Forest

1) Long ago, in the forests of our country, a little girl named Tekakwitha was born. Her father was the chief of the Turtle Clan of the Mohawk nation. Her mother, a gentle woman who believed in Jesus, was of the Algonquin people. When Tekakwitha was four years old, her family all became sick with smallpox. This left little Tekakwitha scarred and with poor eyesight. Her parents died from it. She was raised by her uncle and aunts, and she grew up learning all about the forest animals and plants. Because of her eyes, she did not run and play with the other children, but learned how to do beautiful beadwork. She was quiet and shy, and everyone loved her.

2) Some priests came to her village. Some of the Mohawk people became interested in

learning about Jesus. Many others did not. No one noticed that Tekakwitha, always so quiet, was listening to the stories of Jesus. She was remembering the stories her mother had told her when she was little. And, she was feeling God calling her. When she was a teenager, Tekakwitha asked to be baptized. She had come to love Jesus. She was given another name, Kateri, or Catherine.

3) The others in the village, who did not want to become Christians, did not like Kateri Tekakwitha's decision. They were mean to her. She knew that far away, there was a village of other Mohawk people who were Christians. She decided to go there. She traveled rivers by canoe and forests on foot. After many days, she came to her new home.

4) Now Kateri Tekakwitha could live just as she wanted. She prayed many hours each day. She helped children and older people. Often, she was asked to tell stories of her Mohawk people and about Jesus. The others there found she was very holy. Kateri Tekakwitha had never been strong, and she became very sick and died when she was only twenty-four years old. When she died, the scars from the smallpox left her face and she was as beautiful on the outside as she had always been on the inside.

Celebration Table

In honor of Kateri, cover your table with an earth-tone cloth. Place a picture of Kateri, a picture of Jesus, and a set of children's Bible stories on your table. This will remind the children that Kateri loved to share stories about Jesus and that nothing could keep her from the love of God. Honor Kateri with the beauty of nature by inviting children to add small elements such as twigs, leaves, and nuts to the table.

July 15 – St. Swithun

St. Swithun lived in England in the 800s and was known for his wisdom, knowledge, and humility. His feast day comes at a time when rain is a particular concern—too much or too little will ruin crops. Perhaps because of this, a rhyme is recited on this day in England that has echoes of Ground Hog Day and Candlemas traditions:

St. Swithun's Day, if thou dost rain,
For forty days it will remain.
St. Swithun's Day, if thou be fair,
For forty days 'twill rain nae mair.

July 22 – St. Mary Magdalene

Mary came from a town called Magdala, a small fishing town on the Sea of Galilee. In the Gospel, we learn that Jesus healed her. After that, Mary became one of Jesus' most devoted followers. She and a few other women traveled with Jesus and the apostles so she could learn from Jesus. This was very courageous because women were not usually allowed to study with a teacher, or rabbi. Mary had the courage to stay with Jesus as he was dying. She had the courage to go to his tomb three days later. Because of this, she was the first to hear that Jesus had risen from the dead, and was the first to see him then. In addition to her courage, Mary Magdalene is remembered for how deeply she loved Jesus.

Discussion Starter: What was Mary Magdalene the first to hear?

July 23 – St. Bridget of Sweden

When a person does many jobs, it is said that he "wears many hats." This was very true of Bridget. She was a princess, a person who had visions, a very holy person, a worker for justice, a helper of the poor, a founder of a group of religious people, and the mother of a saint, Catherine of Sweden. Someone who worked for Bridget said that she was always kind and gentle to everyone, and that she had a smiling face!

Activity: *Smiling Discussion*

Talk with children about smiling. Try to help them understand that they have reasons to smile beyond receiving something or feeling happy about something outward. They can also smile to help someone else feel better, to show love, and to be kind and friendly.

July 25 – St. James the Apostle

James and his brother John were fishermen who became Jesus' apostles. They may have been fishing partners with St. Peter and St. Andrew who were also brothers. Jesus called James and John "sons of thunder." James saw many of Jesus' miracles. He was at the Transfiguration, and in the Garden of Gethsemane after the Last Supper. There is a great shrine to James in Spain, where he is called "El Senor Santiago."

Discussion Starter: What did Jesus call St. James and St. John?

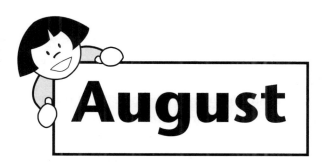

August at a Glance

Dedication for August: Blessed Sacrament

August's Liturgical Color

Patron Saints of the Month

August 6: Feast of the Transfiguration

August 6 & 9: Hiroshima/Nagasaki Memorial Days

August 11: St.Clare

August 15: Assumption of Mary

August 21: Story of Mary

August 22: The Feast of the Queenship of Mary

August 24: St. Bartholomew the Apostle

Dedication for August: Blessed Sacrament

The Blessed Sacrament is the presence of Christ in the Bread of Eucharist. Over the years, people have had special times during prayer with the Blessed Sacrament. The Blessed Sacrament helps us to remember that even when there is not a Mass, Jesus, in the Eucharist, is still present in the church.

Liturgical Color

Ordinary Time: Green

The liturgical color used is green, the color of hope and life.

Patron Saints of the Month

August 8: Dominic: astronomers, Dominican Republic

August 11: Clare: television, television writers

August 16: Stephen of Hungary: Hungary, kings, stonemasons, bricklayers

August 23: Rose of Lima: the Americas

August 28: Augustine: printers, theologians

August 6 – Feast of the Transfiguration

According to Scripture, Peter, James and John witnessed the presentation of the divine glory of Christ. It is believed that Christ wanted to strengthen the faith of the Apostles prior to his death, so that they would know him when he returned. Through this amazing revelation, we recognize Jesus' divinity and hope for our own glory.

Story: What the Apostles Saw (based on Luke 9:28-36)

Jesus took three of his apostles, Peter, James and John, up a mountain. Jesus began to pray, but the others became very sleepy. Then they suddenly realized that Jesus had changed—he had been "transfigured." Now his face and clothes were dazzlingly white!

The apostles looked again and saw Jesus was no longer standing alone. Two great and holy people from long ago, Moses and Elijah, were standing beside the radiant Jesus.

Now the apostles were completely awake! They were very nervous. Peter understood who these important people were and he blurted out, "Lord, it is good we are here. Let us make three tents, one for you, one for Moses, and one for Elijah!"

As he said this, a cloud came and cast a shadow over them. Now the apostles were very frightened. Then, from the cloud came a voice that said, "This is my chosen Son; listen to him."

When the voice was silent, the apostles saw that Elijah and Moses were gone.

Jesus and his apostles went back down the mountain. They did not tell anyone about the vision they had.

When St. Peter offered to make tents, he may have been referring to the Jewish festival called Sukkot when temporary shelters are built. See pages 44-45 for a description of Sukkot.

Discussion Starter: What happened when Jesus began to pray?

August 6 & 9 – Hiroshima and Nagasaki Memorial Days

Among the many tragedies of World War II was the tremendous destruction of life in the bombings of the Japanese cities of Hiroshima and Nagasaki. On that anniversary, the peace park in Hiroshima is filled with people praying for peace. After dark, children set paper lanterns afloat on the Ohta River. Each lantern carries the name of someone who died. As the lanterns drift off, the children sing a song of peace.

Young children can begin to understand the enormous need for world peace, and their ability to pray for it. Set an array of vigil candles, preferably in many colors, on the Celebration Table. Light them all, telling the children the candles honor the many people who died in a huge war. Sit silently for a moment, and then lead the children in praying the "Hail Mary" for peace in the world.

August 11 – St. Clare

Clare was a young, wealthy woman who lived in Assisi, Italy. She knew of the man everyone called Francis, the poor man of Assisi. She knew he had once been rich also, and had nice clothing and much fun with his friends. Now he owned nothing, wore rough clothing, and found all his joy because of God. Clare's aunt took her to hear Francis speak. And through Francis, God spoke to Clare, too. She too gave up all her parties, pretty clothes, and money. She too began to live in poverty and to love Jesus. Many people began to see her holiness and to understand how deeply she loved Jesus. Soon other women joined her, and Clare was their leader. They were called "The Poor Ladies." That was a long time ago. But even today, there are nuns who follow St.

Clare's example, and they are called "The Poor Clares" in her honor.

Story: The Clear Light

A wealthy woman knelt in church. She was expecting a baby, and was praying. Suddenly, she heard a voice saying, "You will give birth to a clear light, which will light up the world!"

Soon after, the woman had a baby girl. Because of the voice she had heard while she had prayed, she named the baby "Chiara," which means "clear one" in Italian.

In English, Chiara is "Clare," and the baby grew to be the holy and joyful St. Clare of Assisi, whose love for Jesus was light to many, many people.

Discussion Starter: How can our love for Jesus help others?

August 15 – Assumption of Mary

"My being proclaims the greatness of the Lord, My spirit finds joy in God my savior." Luke 1:46

The Assumption of Mary is the day we remember the ascension, the going up of Mary, body and soul to heaven. The belief of people ascending into heaven is part of both Jewish and Christian tradition. In 1915 Pope Pius XII proclaimed the Assumption of Mary as official church doctrine. It is a holy day of obligation.

Prayer

Holy Mary, on this day of your ascension into heaven, we honor your life as the chosen Mother of Jesus. We remember your dedication to God and the joy and heartache you had in your life as you followed God's plan for you. Today we pray for the love you had for God, the hope you had in Jesus, and the joy you found in your heart. Pray for us as we grow in love, hope and joy. Amen.

Activities

Prayer to Mary

Pray the Hail Mary or a Rosary in a quiet, outside place today.

Marian Plants

Plant a perennial plant in your church garden to honor Mary. Add a special marker so that you can check for new growth in the spring.

Marian Banners

Make banners for your classroom using the words love, hope and joy. Write each word on a poster board and have the children look through magazines for pictures that illustrate those ideas.

Marian Panel Art

Fold a 12" by 18" piece of construction paper into thirds. Write love on one panel, hope on the next panel and joy on the third. Have the children illustrate each word with drawings or stickers. Send this home as a reminder of Mary and her faith in God.

Traditions

• In the country of Armenia, no one tastes the grapes growing in the vineyards until the Feast of the Assumption. Then, a tray of the new grapes is brought to the church, where they are blessed. After that, everyone enjoys the fruit.

• In southern Brazil, the Feast of the Assumption is also called "Our Lady of the Navigators." To navigate means to steer or guide something like a boat or plane. On this day, people decorate their canoes. They travel to other villages to play music and to enjoy a feast.

August 21 – Story of Mary

In 1879, the people of Ireland were greatly troubled. There had been political fighting, loss of jobs, poor crops, and hunger. People had died. Many others were leaving the country, trying to find a better place to live. In the village of Cnoc, or Knock, the priest had been saying Masses for all the people who had died recently. On August 21 of that year, he said the last of the one hundred Masses. That night, something very wonderful and miraculous happened in Knock. Here is the story:

Story: Our Lady of Knock

It was raining heavily that August evening in the quiet village of Knock. A woman looked out her window. She was startled to see a strange light by the church. She peered through the rain. "It is Mary! The Mother of God!" she cried out.

At another house, a man saw the light too. "Come quickly!" he shouted to anyone who could hear him over the rainfall. "The Mother of God is here, at our church!"

People hurried through the pouring rain to the church. Six-year-old John Curry came running. So did seventy-five-year-old Bridget Trench. In all, fourteen people gathered, standing in the heavy rain to stare at this miracle. There was much to see.

Mary was dressed in a white gown, with a bright gold crown and a golden rose. With her was Joseph, her husband. And with them was the apostle, John the Evangelist. But that was not all! There was also an altar, and a Lamb stood upon it. A large cross hung behind the lamb, and angels moved all around the cross.

While the rain continued to fall, the heavenly figures were not wet. They remained there, hovering a little above the ground, for two hours! Some of the villagers reached out to touch the holy figures, but felt only the church wall behind them.

The people stayed with the holy visitors, praying the rosary. It was a silent night, except for the rain, but one that the people of Knock would never forget!

August 22 – The Feast of the Queenship of Mary

Eight days after the feast of the Assumption, the Church recognizes Mary as "Regina Caeli," the Queen of Heaven.

Prayer

Psalm 45:14 is sung on both of these Marian feasts. Read part of that psalm aloud to the children:

"Ah glorious is the king's daughter as she enters,
her raiment threaded with gold;
In embroidered apparel she is led to the king."

Activity: *Royal Art*

Copy the drawing of the Queenship of Mary on page 174 for each child to color. Make certain you have provided gold crayons!

August 24 – St. Bartholomew the Apostle

St. Bartholomew was among the apostles of Jesus. He was with the others at Pentecost and received the gifts of the Holy Spirit. He later traveled, teaching people in far away lands about Jesus. He is not mentioned often in the Gospels and it may be that Bartholomew was his last name, and Nathaneal was his first name. Nathaneal is mentioned frequently with the apostle, Philip.

Index

Index

Index

Recommended Resources

Favorite Resources for Catholic Customs and Traditions

A Handbook of Catholic Sacramentals, Ann Ball, Our Sunday Visitor

All Saints, Daily Reflections on Saints, Prophets, and Witnesses for Our Time, by Robert Ellsberg, Crossroad Publishing Company

Blessed Kateri and the Cross in the Woods, (Children's storybook) Anne E. Neuberger, Our Sunday Visitor

Building Catholic Family Traditions, Paul and Leisa Thigpen, Our Sunday Visitor

Catholic Customs and Traditions by Greg Dues, Twenty-Third Publications

Catholic Traditions in Cooking, Ann Ball, Our Sunday Visitor

Catholic Traditions in Crafts, Ann Ball, Our Sunday Visitor

Catholic Traditions in the Garden, Ann Ball, Our Sunday Visitor

Christian Beginnings, Volumes, Volumes 1, 2 and 3, Edited by Beth McNamara, Our Sunday Visitor

Enriching Faith through Family Celebrations, Sandra DeGidio, Twenty-Third Publications

Encyclopedia of Catholic Devotions And Practices, Ann Ball, Our Sunday Visitor

Encyclopedia of Saints, Matthew Bunson, Margaret Bunson, and Stephen Bunson, Our Sunday Visitor

Family Countdown to Easter, Debbie Tafton O'Neal, Augsburg Publishing

Follow the Year, Mala Powers, Harper Row

Handbook of Preschool Religious Education, Donald Ratcliff, Religious Education Press

Jesus' Journey: A Lenten Storyboard, Anne E. Neuberger, Our Sunday Visitor

The How-To-Book of Catholic Devotions, Mike Aquilina and Regis J. Flaherty, Our Sunday Visitor

St. Francis and His Feathered Friends, (Children's storybook) Anne E. Neuberger, Our Sunday Visitor

St. Therese in Jesus' Garden, (Children's storybook) Anne E. Neuberger, Our Sunday Visitor

The Catholic Source Book, Rev. Peter Klein, Brown-Roa

Teach Me About Mary, Paul S. Plum, Joan E. Plum, and Catherine M. Odell, Our Sunday Visitor

Teach Me About The Mass, Paul S. Plum, Joan E. Plum, and Catherine M. Odell, Our Sunday Visitor

To Dance With God, Gertrud Mueller Nelson, Paulist Press

Welcome Jesus: An Advent Storyboard, Anne E. Neuberger, Our Sunday Visitor

Why Is That in Tradition?, Patrick Madrid, Our Sunday Visitor

Teaching children about Christian beliefs, attitudes, and values is an awe-inspiring task.

Let us help!

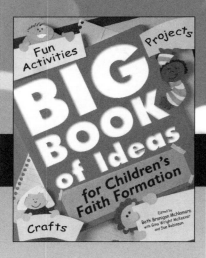

- **Faith-centered**
- **Classroom-tested**
- **Filled with hundreds of fresh ideas**

Our Sunday Visitor's
BIG BOOK of Ideas
for Children's Faith Formation

Easy – Energizing – Effective – NEW

Easy to use with any curriculum, educational materials, or alone. Included materials lists, reproducible patterns, illustrations, and easy-to-follow directions make this resource user-friendly. A comprehensive topic index makes what you are looking for easy to find.

Energizing because teachers and children are fueled with interactive activities, crafts, rhymes, games, and easy-to-sing songs. Quick to prepare and fun to use, there is a multitude of options for various ages, class sizes, and learning styles.

Effective for children and teachers because children learn best when they are able to actively respond. Each idea offers an encounter with faith that children can apply to their lives and won't forget.

**Big Book of Ideas
for Children's Faith Formation**
Edited by Beth Branigan McNamara
with Gina Wright McKeever and Sue Robinson
0-87973-018-8, paper, 352 pp., **$24.95**

Available at bookstores. MasterCard, VISA, and Discover customers can order direct from **Our Sunday Visitor** by calling **1-800-348-2440**. Order online at www.osv.com. Or, send payment **plus** $5.95 shipping/handling fee per order to:

Our Sunday Visitor
200 Noll Plaza • Huntington, IN 46750
1-800-348-2440 • e-mail: osvbooks@osv.com

Our Sunday Visitor